THE SHAME OF HER YOUTH

KATHLEEN HAND WARDER

Pacific Press Publishing Association
Boise, Idaho
Oshawa, Ontario, Canada

Edited by Marvin Moore
Designed by Tim Larson
Cover Photo by Duane Tank
Type set in 10/12 Century Schoolbook

Library of Congress Cataloging in Publication Data

Warder, Kathleen Hand, 1910-
  The shame of her youth.

  1. Remarriage—Religious aspects—Christianity. I. Title.
BV835.W37   1987   261.8'3589   87-2562
ISBN 0-8163-0707-5

87 88 89 90 91 ● 5 4 3 2 1

Contents

Chapter 1
Divorce!

"Divorce Granted!"

Jennie felt the words slam against the wall of the dimly lit, high-vaulted old courtroom, ricocheting back and forth, screaming louder and louder, as if in mockery and accusation. Divorce! . . . Divorce! . . . Divorce!

Judge Reed glanced at the small, crumpled woman in front of him. He guessed her to be about thirty. Dressed in a neat summer frock, her soft dark hair was pulled back and tied loosely with a ribbon. Several strands escaped and lay plastered to her forehead with perspiration. Her large, black-lashed eyes were swollen with weeping. She pulled herself to her feet with an air of utter weariness. The judge leaned over to say a few words to Jennie's attorney. "Confound it!" he thought. "Sometimes I hate this job!" He picked up his gavel. "Next case!"

Jennie felt helpless as she turned. Larry had always been the center of her life. And little Kathy loved her daddy so. Even now, Jennie felt that this must be some horrible dream from which she would soon awaken. How could everyone in Crestview have known of Larry's affair except her? Even when she had gone to her sister Beth's, she found that both she and Bob her husband had known! How could her own sister not have told her? They said they felt she wouldn't believe them and had hoped it would "blow over." She had wanted to scream. "Now, it is over," she sighed, and, lifting her chin, she walked dry-eyed from the courtroom. A bus was waiting at the corner, and she stumbled blindly to it. It dropped her off only a short distance from where she had left Kathy. Beth was waiting with a plate of fresh cookies and a tall glass of cold milk. Kathy was happily involved with her cousin, Janie, and greeted her casually. In a daze Jennie refused the refreshments, somehow feeling a vague resentment at Beth, so secure in her husband's love.

Jennie could never remember how she spent the next few weeks. Her heart was heavy with the thought of a lifetime without Larry, and she harbored a building resentment against the woman who had taken him away.

Mornings she helped Kathy dress and prepared her breakfast, listening all the while to the five-year old's chatter. Kathy was a vivacious child, small for her age, but a hurricane of energy, and her dancing blue eyes missed nothing. Only occasionally did Jennie notice the deep scar left by her father's desertion. After breakfast, Jennie would drop Kathy off at the nursery school on her way to work in a small factory that manufactured men's dress shirts. Working frantically at her sewing machine, she had no time for her personal problems. By sheer determination, she kept a light, playful attitude and hid her heavy heart from Kathy.

Jennie's nights were searing agony, tormented with visions of Larry and his new love. Gradually she would realize that her body was drawn into a knot and would force her muscles to relax. Sometimes, toward the morning, she would fall into an exhausted, troubled sleep, but many nights she did not sleep at all.

Sundays helped, for Jennie loved the services at her home church in Crestview. The familiar hymns were a balm to her bruised heart. The concerned faces of her friends and their smiles of encouragement were a source of strength. Even here, though, she was reminded of the years she and Larry had spent together singing in the choir and working in the Sunday School. They had grown up here and had been childhood sweethearts here. So the days ground on.

One night as Jennie sat in the tiny living room mending a blouse, she heard Kathy's small voice.

"Mommy!"

The child had been in bed for hours, and Jennie supposed that she had dropped off to sleep long ago. Frightened, she hurried to see what was wrong. Kathy was sitting up in bed, her soft blond curls tousled around her face, her big eyes full of tears.

"What is it, Sweetheart? I thought you were asleep."

A chubby fist rubbed away a tear. "Well, I just thought that I've been askin' and askin' Jesus to bring my daddy back. Why doesn't He do it?"

Jennie swallowed a lump in her throat. "And I thought she had forgotten," she scolded herself. Sweeping the child into her arms, she questioned silently, "Yes, why don't You bring him back, Lord?" Aloud she said, "I guess we must wait a bit longer, honey."

A rocking chair and a crooning little song soon comforted the little girl, but Jennie lay awake until dawn before she fell into a troubled sleep. For what would she finally tell her baby if Daddy *never* came home?

Three years later, everything about those first agonizing months after the divorce was hazy. Like a robot Jennie had gone through the dreary daily routine, desperately trying to maintain an outward calm for Kathy's sake, but inside she was bruised and bleeding.

Only a few things stood out in her mind. One memory she would never forget was the hot August day she met her Sunday School teacher, Mrs. Sand, downtown. Mrs. Sand had told her hesitatingly that word had come that Larry was married and that he and his new wife had gone to California! Jennie could still feel the searing agony, the frantic fighting for breath. She had fainted right on the sidewalk. One evening she had planned to commit suicide, but Mr. and Mrs. Sand stopped by for a visit and saved her from that terrible mistake.

Although she spent the holidays that year with Beth and Bob, she was surrounded by an aching loneliness. Her parents had come from their home in Chicago and urged her to come live with them. None of these things seemed to help much. The dismal daily tasks went on.

The turning point came one evening when she and Beth had been dawdling over a plate of Beth's cookies and Beth suggested that she rethink her parents' invitation to go to Chicago.

"If you have to work," Beth said, "I wish you could have a better job—one with more promise and not so hard. In Chicago you could go to business college at night."

"Well, I don't know, maybe I should," Jennie replied.

"And another thing, Jen—and I've mentioned this to you before—Bob and I want you to know that we hope someday you will marry again." Beth hesitated, for she knew how almost fanatical her sister was on the subject. "You are so young and pretty. I just can't believe the Lord would expect you to pay for Larry's infidelity all your life and let him go scot-free!"

Jennie glanced at Beth without the resentment with which she had always greeted the subject before. "I must admit that I think of it occasionally, but my mind goes in circles. I know divorce is never God's perfect plan. He meant it to be one man and one woman until death, but it does take two working together to keep the commitment. Oh, I don't know. I feel so confused when I try to sort it all out. I don't think divorce solves any problems. It just creates more, so I have just decided to concentrate on Kathy for now and wait and see how the Lord leads. I *think* I am willing to be alone, and I *do* want to do His will more than anything, but it is so hard," she sighed. "I guess I am a woman who needs a man, not just a career woman."

That was the beginning of the change. In no time, it seemed, Jennie found herself making arrangements for the move to Chicago—packing, sorting, and preparing to say goodbye to life-long friends before leaving Crestview, where she had lived much of her life and where part of her heart would always be.

Chicago was a nightmare. She held an evening job from three o'clock till midnight, then dashed for a streetcar to bring her home for a few hours of sleep. Mornings she tried to snatch a few precious moments with Kathy before sending her off to school and catching the El (short for Chicago's elevated railway) downtown to her own classes. One day she began to have dizzy spells. Once she fainted on the El platform. She made a quick trip to a doctor who told her that she was on the verge of exhaustion and must have some rest. She felt disgusted and angry. "To think that I spent money I can ill afford to be told something I already know," she muttered as she left his office.

Two life-changing letters arrived in the mail just one day apart. One was from an old friend, Eileen Winter. Eileen had been born and raised in Crestview, and she and Jennie had been "best friends," almost inseparable, until Eileen married and moved to Sioux City, Iowa. Over the years they had corresponded faithfully. Now Eileen wrote that she wished Jennie and Kathy would come to them. Jobs were plentiful, and they would help her find an apartment. Jennie yearned to make the change, but knew she did not have the money for such a big move.

The next day brought a letter from the Department of the Army stating in stilted terms that Lawrence Shelby had enlisted in the army and in the near future she would be receiving a monthly allowance for their dependent child! Larry had been ordered to make monthly child-support payments, at the time of the divorce, but he had never complied. Could this be the Lord's provision for the move to Iowa?

All these memories churned in Jennie's mind as the plane flew through the darkness, taking her and Kathy to Sioux City, and a whole new life. It had been three years since she stood in that courtroom and heard those horrible words that had changed their lives so drastically.

"Here I am, thirty-three years old, and have been divorced almost three years," she thought. "I've only mended a little. I've grieved far too long. I must learn to accept my life as it is."

Reaching over, she touched eight-year-old Kathy, who was curled up in the seat beside her sound asleep. She smiled softly. "What a wonderful companion she has become. Even though she rebelled a little about leaving her school and friends, she boarded the plane without a tear.

"Lord, help me to follow Your leading that simply," Jennie prayed silently. The verse from her morning devotions came clearly to her mind:

The Lord God is a sun and shield: the Lord will give grace and glory: no good thing will he withhold from them that walk uprightly. Psalm 84:11.

"Ah, there is it," she thought. "No *good* thing will He withhold. So if He withholds a husband, I must accept it and know it would not be good for me, at least not now."

At long last Jennie's heart was at peace.

Jennie liked Sioux City at once. She stepped off the plane into a brightly lighted modern-looking terminal. "Things will be better here," she thought.

Eileen and Roger were waiting. Jennie had met Roger briefly on one of their quick trips back to Crestview, but she felt strange with him. However, in his charming way he soon put her at ease. Eileen was still beautiful. Her stylish and obviously expensive clothes set off her gleaming blond hair and deep brown eyes. Her flawless skin and delicately molded face were still the same, yet Jennie noticed that something was missing—an inner glow. As they laughed together and "remembered," Jennie was aware of a haunted look deep in Eileen's eyes.

In no time, it seemed, they had covered the five miles from the airport into Sioux City. Roger pointed out various points of interest as they drove through town. Jennie felt eager for the future.

"I'll be teaching again this year," Eileen said, "but Roger's mother lives with us, and she'll be glad to give Kathy her lunch should you decide to stay with us after school starts."

"Oh no, thank you, but we must find our own place just as quickly as possible," Jennie replied. "I can't tell you how I appreciate your having us for a few weeks," she added hurriedly, "but I think Kathy needs her own home."

"You don't know what you are asking," Eileen mused. "I have found the apartment situation almost impossible. But Roger knows a lot of influential people, so that should help."

"I *must* get a job in a week or so," Jennie added, "and we should be settled before school starts."

The two woman talked on long after Kathy was asleep in one of the twin beds in Eileen's beautiful guest room. After a few days of just visiting, Jennie began her job hunting in earnest, for she was painfully aware that her money was running very low.

The papers were full of available openings. After two interviews, she accepted employment in the stenographic pool of a nationally known rubber company. The salary was not as much as she had hoped for, but they promised her a raise in three months, and the location was good.

"I start work on Monday," she told Eileen happily that evening as they finished the dishes. "Now I must look for an apartment."

Eileen rinsed out the dish cloth and hung it up. "Yes, but that won't be as easy as finding a job, I'm afraid."

"I know," Jennie agreed, "but the Lord brought us here, of that I am sure, and He will not desert us now."

Eileen turned quickly. "On, Jen, are you still that religious?" But before Jennie could answer, she added hurriedly, "Oh, I must hurry and change. I'm meeting some friends at the country club later. Sorry." And she was gone.

Whether she imagined it or not, Jennie felt that the situation at Eileen's was becoming a little strained. Eileen was still cordial, but both Roger and his mother remained distant and slightly disapproving. Neither appeared for breakfast one morning. Jennie ate in embarrassed haste, hurrying Kathy more than was comfortable because of the growing tension.

As the time for the beginning of school approached, Jennie became somewhat frantic, but she hid her feelings from Kathy. Each day she spent her lunch hour in the phone booth outside the office calling every apartment rental ad in the paper, but with no success.

One Saturday morning Jennie and Kathy decided to eat their lunch together at a nearby park. They had just set their lunch on one of the picnic tables when an elderly couple came up and asked, since all the tables were full, if they could share the space at Jenny and Kathy's table. They introduced themselves as Mr. and Mrs. Fisher, and in no time they were all chatting like old friends. They loved Kathy at once, and compared her to their granddaughter, who lived many miles away. Jennie warmed toward them when she learned that they attended the little church just a couple of blocks down the street, and accepted their invitation to meet them there for services the next day. Jennie confided in them her need to find an apartment, and they assured her that it would not be easy, but promised to "ask around." They parted, reminding one another they would meet again at church.

After church the following day, the Fishers invited Jennie and Kathy to their home for lunch. It was a pleasant little house, and for the first time since arriving in Sioux City, Jennie felt that she was with her own kind of people.

"You know, Jennie," Mrs. Fisher said after lunch, "when Dad and I got home last night after meeting you in the park, we got to talking about your need for an apartment. I know how very difficult that will be and I have no suggestions, really, but it does happen that we have an extra room we could rent for a few weeks if that would help. We have never rented a room, but our son Jack has been sent by his company to Europe, and his room will be empty until after Christmas.

Jennie was interested at once, so Mrs. Fisher showed her the room. It was a large bedroom that had been furnished with a large desk and lounge chair. It had an alcove, an entrance, and bath that had been added for the young man's convenience.

Jennie was delighted, and it didn't take them long to make arrangements for the move. Kathy squealed with joy. "Oh, Mom, let's move right now! They've got a dog and everything." The Fishers offered to get their son-in-law to help them with his truck, but Jennie assured them that she and Kathy had only a few things.

The following weekend Jennie thanked Roger and Eileen for the kind hospitality during her first few weeks in Sioux City and moved into the spare room in the Fisher's home.

Chapter 2
The Miracle Apartment

The next few months were so busy that Jennie almost forgot she must find an apartment. Their arrangement with the Fishers worked out very well, and Kathy quickly made friends among the neighborhood children. The worst inconvenience was that when Jennie arrived home tired and disheveled after a day's work and a long ride on the bus, she and Kathy had to walk several blocks to the little lunch room where they had their evening meal. Jennie knew that this was not a satisfactory way to feed a growing child.

Jennie soon discovered that money was a constant problem. Eating out every day was very expensive, and it was a battle to keep Kathy in clothes. There was no denying that she was a growing child. It seemed that each evening some garment had to be repaired or lengthened. Her shoes would soon have to be replaced, her dresses were too short, and her coat was so snug across the shoulders that it couldn't be altered. Jennie faced the problem of new clothes for Kathy at once, and found everything a strain on her purse. She somehow contrived an adequate wardrobe for school (her own clothes would just have to do) and spent many evenings remodeling old things to look as nice as possible.

Jennie soon became friendly with one of the girls at the office, and they often had lunch together. Frances Johnson had a plump, pretty face and a heart as gay as her dancing gray eyes. She was engaged to a young man in the army and talked of nothing but the time when he would be home on a furlough long enough for them to get married.

"Jennie," she said one morning as they were walking to their desks, "I want to be sure and talk to you today."

"OK, let's have lunch together. We can eat at the Green Parrott since this is payday," Jennie suggested.

Later, after the two young women were seated in their favorite eating place, Frances said, "I hope you won't think I'm sticking my nose into your business, Jen, but I know you want to get another place to live and I may have a solution."

"If you could, it would be an answer to prayer," Jennie assured her.

"I can't imagine being the answer to anyone's prayer, but I do have an idea," Frances giggled. "You know that I am going to be married one of these days, just as soon as Jim can get a ten-day pass. Well, I've had a little three-room apartment for several years. I share it with another girl, but the lease is in my name. The plan has always been that when I got married Alice, my roommate, would take over my lease, and it would be her apartment. Now, something new has come up. Alice had decided to get married in a couple of months and move to the farm, so I will need another roommate, and I thought of you. I talked to the landlady, as they do not ordinarily take children, but they will make an exception with Kathy." She paused to take a sip of water.

"Fran, this is a miracle! I can hardly believe it! Of course, I'm interested. In fact I'm flabbergasted." Jennie's eyes glowed.

"There's one hitch, though," Frances said. "You would have to move in before Alice moves out, and it will be pretty crowded for a few weeks. Also, your little girl will have to change schools."

Jennie's heart sank. "Oh dear, I forgot I would have to have someone to care for Kathy during the day when she gets home from school," she sighed. "I don't know. It's a wonderful opportunity."

Frances puckered her brow and thought aloud. "Yes, that is something, but—well, maybe I can work *that* out too."

They turned the plan over as they walked leisurely back to the office, and Fran said, "Let me look around and let you know tomorrow. I would like to have you for my roommate. It may be a year before Jim comes home, and I like children."

Jennie's mind was in a whirl all afternoon, and she could hardly wait to get home and tell Kathy the news.

"But Mommy, I already have friends here," Kathy protested.

"I know, Honey, and I hate to always be dragging you from

place to place, but you can make new friends. I hope we will be settled this time."

Mrs. Fisher was amazed. "Jennie, I wonder if you realize what a miracle this is! I know plenty of folks with lots of money who have not been able to buy or steal the tiniest apartment."

"All I can say is that it is a direct answer to prayer," Jennie said quietly and Mrs. Fisher agreed.

The next morning Frances greeted Jennie with a big smile. "I think I found a baby sitter, Jen. Last night I asked my landlady, Mrs. Carpenter, about it, and she offered to watch Kathy for you after school. She is a widow and lives right across the hall with her semi-invalid son. He helps her a little with the work, but can't do much."

Jennie hesitated, "Fran, knowing you, I can take the apartment sight unseen, but I would feel better if I could meet Mrs. Carpenter before I agree to turn Kathy's care over to her."

Frances smiled. "I thought that was what you would say, so I have already made plans for you to come over for lunch on Saturday. You can meet Alice and see the apartment too."

When Saturday finally came and they took the bus to the apartment, they were pleasantly surprised about everything. Mrs. Carpenter proved to be a small, quiet woman who loved children. She and Kathy became friends at once. The apartment building was old, but well kept, and Frances' place was on the first floor.

The apartment consisted of a large living room, a bedroom, a small dining area, and a tiny kitchen. A large walk-in closet in the living room contained a foldaway bed, built in drawers, and storage space for clothing. They agreed that until Alice was married she and Frances would use the twin beds in the bedroom and Kathy and Jennie the foldaway bed.

"Thank You, Lord," Jennie breathed as they walked the two blocks from the bus stop to the Fishers' home. Kathy skipped ahead, bursting with the good news.

Suddenly a new thought struck Jennie like a dash of cold water. "Furniture! I don't have any furniture, and when Alice and Fran are gone they will take theirs with them." Her heart sank, but only for a moment. A small voice in her said, "The Lord supplied the apartment. Don't you think He can furnish it too?"

It was with a feeling of deep contentment that Jennie helped her little girl get ready for bed that night. "Truly the Lord is good," she thought as she drifted off to sleep, not even realizing that she hadn't thought of Larry for weeks.

They moved on a cold, blustering day in early December. The air was full of swirling snow, but the apartment was warm and bright, and there was much laughter and jostling as they dashed around, juggling closet and drawer space. Dinner was served with a special flourish to celebrate the occasion. Fran and Jennie spent the evening sharing the pint-sized bathroom for baths and shampoos. "I want to find a church within walking distance, if possible," Jennie said.

"Yeah, I thought of that." Fran's mouth was full of bobby pins. "I know you are religious, but I can't help you there, I'm afraid. There is a little church of some kind down on Thirteenth Street a couple of blocks."

It was bitter cold the next morning as Jennie hurried through the snowy streets to church. Kathy skipped along beside her, their breath making little blue rings in the frigid air. They slipped quickly into the warm, pleasant church and found seats at the back during a familiar old hymn: "A Mighty Fortress Is Our God."

Jennie smiled to herself, and a warm, happy feeling enfolded her. An usher slipped over quietly and invited Kathy to junior church, so Jennie was free to give her full attention to the sermon. It was an inspiring service, and the people were warm and friendly. The young pastor greeted them after church, inviting them back for the evening service.

Jennie's heart was light as they walked home. Kathy chattered gleefully all the way about a girl she met who would be in her class at the new school. "I have a friend already, Mother," she bubbled, jumping over a pile of hard-crusted snow.

Jennie's mind was on plans for their lunch as they burst into the warm apartment from the bitter cold. It had been agreed that on Sunday each one would make her own lunch, but before she could get her coat off Fran called from the dining room. "Hurry! hurry! Come in here. I have news!" She was sitting at the table, her round face glowing, her hair still in curlers. Looking up she grinned, pouring Jennie and Kathy each a cup of hot chocolate left over from her breakfast.

"Sit!" she commanded, pointing to an empty chair. "I have terrific news."

Jennie sat, and Kathy watched the dramatic scene questioningly.

"I'm so excited," Fran crowed. "I just got a call from Jim and he's on his way home. He'll arrive tomorrow, and we will be married next week. Before you get settled, Jen, I'll be gone! Oh, joy! How's that for timing?"

Jennie caught her breath, then burst out laughing. "Isn't it amazing how the Lord works?"

"I don't know about the Lord's part in it, but it sure worked out perfectly, didn't it?" Fran replied. And here we thought Alice would be leaving first!"

The next few days were a mad rush to get everything done on time, but Frances was able to have her church wedding with Alice as maid of honor.

Watching the happy couple leave for California in Jim's old car brought a stab of pain to Jennie's heart. Most of the time she kept so busy that she seldom thought of her own loss, but the glimpse of a shared intimate look still hurt. "Lord, help me not to be jealous," she breathed.

As the weeks slipped by, Jennie and Kathy settled into a routine with Alice, but they knew it was only temporary. Alice spent most of her spare time at her parent's home in the country planning a beautiful church wedding.

The week after Fran left a truck came and picked up the rest of her things, which included all the living room furniture, leaving that room bare except for the carpet. Alice would take the bedroom things, leaving only a folding table and two rickety chairs in the dining room. Jennie began to realize that the time was very near when she would have to find her own furniture, and she felt tempted to panic. "Lord, You found me this place," she prayed. "You can find me the furniture, because I have no idea where it's going to come from or how I'll pay for it."

Jennie still called Mrs. Fisher often, and she mentioned one day that she would need to buy some furniture. She asked if Mrs. Fisher knew of a reliable second-hand store in town.

"You know, Jennie," Mrs. Fisher exclaimed, "I never thought of you, but Dad is buying a new living room set for me as a Christmas gift, and the trade-in value is so small that I would rather you had it, if you are interested."

Jennie was overjoyed, remembering the nice things that the Fishers had in their home. "Oh, that would be wonderful!" She replied. "Of course I'm interested. How much would you want for them?"

"If you can get a truck and take them away from here, they're yours."

Jennie insisted on paying, but finally agreed to accept the furniture as a Christmas gift. Soon the familiar couch and chair sat in her apartment. "Now just a lamp or two and a couple of tables, maybe someday another chair," Jennie mused happily. "Nothing needs to be done about the bedroom furniture until March after Alice's wedding."

Christmas was a little sad that year, but they had a small tree and a nice dinner, and Kathy got the bicycle she had been asking for. They had been invited to the Fishers for supper that evening, and as they were saying goodbye Mrs. Fisher handed her an envelope which she said was for an "almost daughter," but not to open it until she got home. Jennie was thrilled to find a check for $25, which she used to buy a second-hand dinette set.

Jennie had enough living room and dining room furniture to get by, but she was still worried about bedroom furniture, especially the beds. Alice's wedding was just three weeks away.

"Did you know about the big furniture sale across the river?" Alice asked at the supper table one night. "They might have something in the way of beds."

Jennie took a bus across the river that same night. The simplest beds she could find that seemed worth getting were $55 apiece even with a sizeable discount. With the tax she would have to pay about $120 for the two of them.

"I need them desperately," she said to the sales lady who waited on her, "but I simply do not have $120, and I don't know any way to get it."

"We have a credit plan," the clerk said. "Why don't you apply at our credit department?"

Jennie's hands trembled as she filled out the papers. "Lord, I don't know how I can afford monthly payments on my tight budget. I don't know whether to ask you to help this application to be approved or rejected."

The application was approved, with payments set at $20 a month for six months. Jennie's mouth felt dry when she signed the papers, but she knew she had no choice. At home that evening she refigured her budget and found a way to squeeze it in. "Help me to have no crises for the next six months," Jennie prayed as she lay in bed that night.

The next morning at the office she was told that her boss, Mr. Ingersoll, wanted to see her in his office. In fear and trembling she seated herself in the chair in front of his desk.

"Good morning, Jennie," he said glancing up from his papers. "I believe you have been with us about six months?"

She swallowed. "Yes, just six months last week." Her voice shook and her hands were tightly clenched in her lap. "What if I lose my job?" she thought.

Mr. Ingersoll picked up a sheaf of papers and read them for a bit while Jennie sat, her heart beating in her throat, and her eyes searching his face for a clue to his purpose.

"Yes, six months last week," her voice shook.

At last Mr. Ingersoll looked up and smiled. "Well, I have a very good report of your work. You have done a nice job. Some of the men prefer your work to that of the other girls, so, we have slated you for a raise in salary. Beginning today you will receive $5 more each week, and if this continues the raise will be repeated in another three months."

Jennie went back to her desk with her heart singing, but it was not until she sat at the dining table that evening in the quiet of her apartment, figuring her monthly budget, that she realized that the raise exactly covered the payment for the furniture she had bought. Once more the Lord had supplied just what she needed, *when* she needed it! "How can I *ever* doubt?" she scolded herself silently.

Chapter 3
Teenage Tenants

Jennie was chosen to train the girl who took Fran's place, and the next few weeks were extremely busy. Dorothy Clements was a tiny redheaded ball of energy, who, having just escaped the dull life of the farm, was determined to live the new life to the hilt. Her mind was sharp and she learned quickly, but she was so much more interested in what went on around her than in the job at hand that Jennie constantly needed to prod her along. Dotty was a lovable scamp. Her throaty laugh and quick wit livened up the whole office.

The evenings were pleasant too. Kathy and Jennie grew very close as they laughed and worked together. When Kathy accepted Christ as her Saviour, Jennie decided that the time had come to move their membership to the church they had been attending. The people welcomed them warmly and quickly invited her to teach a Sunday School class.

Jennie's class was made up of sixteen-year-old girls, all of whom became very dear to her. She spent many hours each week preparing her lesson. The study and prayer challenged her own life, and she determined to be not only a good teacher but a good example.

Always in the back of Jennie's mind, however, was the necessity of finding someone to share the apartment with them. She began to inquire among the people she knew at work. The time for payment of another month's rent was approaching, and Jennie felt a little frantic at the thought. "I can manage this month, but before another one goes by I must have someone," she told herself.

"Did you ever find a roommate?" Dotty asked one morning as she stood near Jennie's desk, sorting invoices.

"Not yet, but I must try to get someone this month."

"Would you want to take two girls instead of one?" Dotty asked casually with a probing glance.

"Wel-l-l, I don't know. I might. It would depend on the girls, I guess."

Dotty concentrated on her task for a minute, then raised her head. "I know a couple of girls from down home, just out of high school, who want to come up here and get jobs. Their folks won't let them come unless they can find a good place to stay."

This was a completely new thought to Jennie. She had planned to find a mature person who would be a companion as well as help with finances. She hesitated. "I could talk to them, I guess. I do have Kathy to think of."

Dotty seemed to relax. "Tell you what I'll do. I'll call my folks tonight and ask them to have these girls come up Saturday for an interview."

That night Jennie told Kathy the plan, and Kathy was interested at once. "Will they play with me?" she asked thoughtfully.

"Oh, no. They'll have to work, so they'll get jobs and be gone most of the time," Jennie explained. "But they'll be here evenings."

She was pleasantly surprised when the young ladies came. Joan Smithers and Jan Goetz had been chums since childhood, and although they were not related, they looked much alike. Both girls were tall, blond, and very thin. They wore tight jeans and T-shirts that matched.

Mrs. Smithers came along to look the place over and see what "the kids" were getting into. She was a dumpy woman with a little black hat perched on top of her gray hair. Her hair was drawn back tightly into a small knot on her neck. Her sharp eyes darted here and there, seeing everything, and her tiny mouth was pulled into a tight, thin line. Her voice was too loud. Neither she nor the Goetzes were very happy about the girls living in the city, but had agreed to let them try it if they could find a suitable place. The fact that both mothers were cautious seemed like a good omen to Jennie.

"Pa and me don't like this very good," Mrs. Smithers said with a cracked voice, "but the girls are so set on it we decided to let them try."

Jennie showed them the arrangements she had in mind. The girls would use the foldaway bed so that Kathy could get to bed at her regular early hour, and they were to keep the apartment neat. Jennie would do the planning and cooking. The girls were to take their laundry home each weekend and always be gone on Saturdays and Sundays.

Joan and Jan decided to go home, and get their things and move in the next day. They arrived in a rush of giggles and a great deal of banging doors and stamping feet. They were accompanied by Jan's father and a couple of boys their own age. Mr. Goetz was a big, muscular man, still dressed in the overalls and heavy shoes he wore to work on his farm. Jennie could not remember his saying a word, not even goodbye, as he drove away in a rusty old pickup.

A mantle of strangeness seemed to drop over the apartment as the girls whispered and giggled, putting their things away in the drawers Jennie had emptied for them.

"Come on out and have some hot chocolate," Jennie called from the dining room, hoping to help them overcome their embarrassment. They came, dragging their feet and with sullen looks. Kathy gathered up her crayons and coloring book, and they all sat around the small table. The hot drink was good, and cheese and crackers made a light meal.

"Would you girls like to go to church with us tonight?" Jennie invited brightly.

A sly look flashed between them, as Jan replied, "No, not tonight, Mrs. Shelby. We have to get ready to go job hunting tomorrow."

That night when Jennie and Kathy came home from church they found the girls sprawled out on the living room floor, clad only in their pajamas, and with the radio blaring.

Jennie's heart sank. How could she ask them to turn down the radio without being insulting? At that moment the phone rang. It was the tenant on the third floor asking "why in Sam Hill" she had to have her radio so loud. She apologized meekly and said she would turn it down at once. Her hands were trembling as she approached the living room.

"Girls, will you please turn the radio down? The man on the third floor just called complaining."

"Oh, phooey! We always have the radio loud," Joan said. "I like it that way."

"That's all right in the country, but in an apartment building we must think of the other people too," Jennie explained patiently. "Also, we must turn it off completely at eleven p.m. That is a condition of my lease."

"Brother! are we going to have all kinds of rules here too?" Jan asked, raising her shoulders in a gesture of disgust.

"I'm afraid you will find that life is full of rules and regulations," Jennie said softly as she reached over and turned down the noise of the screeching little box.

By morning the sun was out, and things looked a little more cheerful. Both Jan and Joan came to breakfast in their pajamas with their hair still in curlers, but it was nice to have their chatter, and they were pleasant with Kathy.

Jennie reminded them that supper would be at six and that they must let her know by noon if they did not plan to eat at home. They nodded.

Getting Kathy off for school and leaving for the office, Jennie felt a strange reluctance leaving with the girls still there, but she had to catch the 8:10 bus.

Each evening when she came home, it was Jennie's custom to stop at Mrs. Carpenter's for Kathy before going into her own place.

"Heard a lot of commotion over at your place last night," was Mrs. Carpenter's first remark. Jennie explained the episode of the radio.

"I'm afraid I may have made a mistake in taking those girls," she admitted.

"Well, I like you Mrs. Shelby, and I hope you won't keep them if they don't quiet down, for if people start complaining we will both be in trouble," she said.

There was one happy time that week. On Wednesday evening Jennie had planned a get-together for her Sunday School class. They met at the church fellowship hall for games, a short devotion, and food. As they gathered in a circle, holding hands for a prayer before going home, one of the girls spoke up. "Mrs. Shelby, I just wanted to tell you that you are a neat teacher. I just love Sunday School now, and I hope you will be our teacher always!"

Before Jennie realized what was happening, they all swarmed around, hugging her and echoing Marie's sentiments.

Entering their apartment one evening a few days later, Jennie noticed that the breakfast dishes were not done—they were not even cleared off the table—and the foldaway bed had not been put up. Jennie's temper flared, and she stopped right in the middle of the room, biting her lip.

"Are you mad, Mom?" Kathy asked.

"Well, let's just say I am very disappointed."

Jennie had her feelings under control by the time the apartment was restored and supper put on the table.

The girls had not come home by 6:15, so she and Kathy went ahead and ate their supper. Just as they were finishing they heard car doors slamming and loud voices in front of the house then the clatter of footsteps on the stairs. The girls blew into the apartment like a young hurricane, strewing their wraps all the way to the dining room.

"I'm afraid your dinner is getting cold." Jennie said in as pleasant a voice as she could summon.

"Oh, that's all right; we already ate," Jan called as she slammed into the bathroom.

"Lord, help me to handle this right," Jennie prayed silently. "I know I got myself into this because I was in such a hurry, and I'm sorry. Please show me what to do now." She waited till the girls were ready for bed, then approached them cautiously.

"Girls," she said, trying to sound both firm and kind at the same time, "we have to have a talk. I don't want to be hard-boiled nor spoil your fun, but there are rules here that must be followed."

She went carefully over all the things they had discussed when the girls first moved in. The girls sat with their heads down, refusing to meet her eyes. Their angry silence hung over the apartment all evening, and the next morning the girls left without eating any breakfast.

Jennie turned the situation over in her mind all day and decided she would ask them to move. Now that they had jobs they could manage something else. But it was with fear and trembling that she faced them that evening.

"I don't think this is going to work out, girls, and I would like to have you look for someplace else.

"You can't make us move. We already paid you." Jan tossed her head defiantly.

"I will give you till the end of the month, but by then I will expect you to have another place."

"There aren't any other places, 'cause we looked." Joan said.

"Then you'll have to go back home." Jennie's voice was firm.

"Oh, please Mrs. Shelby, we'll do anything you say. We just can't go back to that old farm!" Jan's voice was a whine now.

"I'm truly sorry, but I can't," Jennie said as she turned and walked out, closing the door softly.

The next few days were uneventful, and the girls seemed to calm down a good bit. They formed the habit of telling Jennie in the mornings they would not be in for dinner. Usually they came in about nine o'clock, windblown and giggly.

The quiet evenings were a reprieve, and Jennie and Kathy made the most of them. One evening while Jennie was sitting at the dining room table writing letters, Kathy came in carrying a small magazine. "Can I read this book?" she asked.

"May I?" Jennie corrected absently as she took the little magazine in her hand. She glanced at it and felt instantly repulsed. It was filled with the vilest pornographic pictures. She was furious, and for an instant her impulse was to hurl it against the wall.

"Where did you get this?" she demanded, not realizing how angry she looked. Kathy began to whimper. "On the couch, Mommy, but I didn't look at it yet." The little girl's chin was quivering.

Instantly contrite, Jennie took Kathy in her arms. "Oh, Honey, I'm not mad at you." Her arms tightened around the child. "We don't want that kind of thing in our house, and I was very surprised."

Kathy soon forgot the matter as she busied herself with something else, but Jennie was furious.

The girls came in later than usual that night and came in more quietly. Jennie went into the living room to meet them, bolstered by her seething anger.

"Oh, hello Mrs. Shelby," Jan said pleasantly.

Jennie held out the magazine, her eyes snapping. "Who does this belong to?" She asked crisply.

Both girls shrugged as they glanced at the magazine. "Well, er, I guess it belongs to both of us," Jan replied guardedly.

"You are both old enough to know better than this. My little girl reads extremely well, and I will *not* have this filth in my house!" Jennie turned to walk out of the room. The girls had not replied when she turned back. "This is the end. I will refund the rest of the money, and you get out by Friday! That gives you two days to pack. Suit yourselves where you go, but go!" She turned and walked out.

On Friday morning a much-abashed Jan came asking for a few more days. They hadn't found anything yet, but would go anyway by Monday or Tuesday.

Jennie sighed. "I will give you one more week, but that is absolutely all. We get on one another's nerves, and there is no point in prolonging it."

The next day the girls left for a weekend at home. Jennie and Kathy were invited to the Fishers for supper and went happily early in the afternoon. Mr. and Mrs. Fisher were appalled at the situation with their tenants and assured them that the girls must move before they caused more trouble. It was a pleasant evening, and Jennie and Kathy went home happier than they had come.

Walking the last block, Jennie thought she heard loud music, and as she approached the building she noticed the lights were on in her apartment.

"Mom, there is someone in our house," Kathy said, her eyes wide with surprise.

They quickened their pace, and opening the front door of the apartment were confronted with a sight that Jennie could scarcely believe. The rug had been rolled up, and three or four couples were dancing to the loud, heavy beat of music from the radio. Empty beer cans were everywhere. The young people stopped at once, and everyone turned to Jennie as Joan and Jan came forward slowly.

"We came back sooner than we planned," Jan said, testing her reaction.

"Either you gather up your things and get out of here at once, or I will call the police!" Jennie said through tight lips, pronouncing every word carefully. The other young people quickly vanished, leaving Joan and Jan to face her alone. They looked at her sullenly for a moment.

"My dad says you can't put us out," Joan said belligerently.

"Your dad doesn't know me!" Jennie replied crisply. There were several empty boxes on the floor. Jennie began to pull things out of the closet and put them into the girls' boxes. Stunned, they actually obeyed her when she told them to get the clothing out of the drawers and get them packed.

"Where can we go?" Jan whined.

Jennie folded and packed for a moment before answering. "You can always go home, or you can go to a hotel, but you will not stay here another night."

An hour later, after they had finished packing, Jennie went to the phone and called a cab. Then she counted out the correct amount of refund for each girl. She set their luggage out in the hall, then turned to them. "Please give me back my keys. Your cab will be here in a few minutes. I hope you learned as much from this experience as I have, and I wish you well in finding another place." She ushered them into the hall before closing and locking the door.

A smile of relief flirted with the corners of her mouth as she dropped wearily into a chair. "I bet I surprised them," she chuckled, only slightly ashamed of her flare of temper, "but believe me, the next person to move in here will be more carefully chosen!"

Chapter 4
Maggie and Earl

Sunday afternoon Jennie spent an hour figuring her finances and found that by careful planning and some sacrificing they could manage alone for about a month while she looked for another roommate. She determined that this time the person must be congenial and mature enough to not need a chaperon. She knew that if she advertised in the newspaper the number of applicants would be overwhelming, but it was the best way. At the risk of sounding stuffy, her add read:

> Christian lady wanted to share apartment.
> Must be fond of children.

All the way to work on Monday Jennie wondered how she would tell Dotty about the end of her arrangement with the girls without offending. As it turned out, she need not have given it a thought, for when she told her what had happened Dotty threw back her head and laughed merrily, "Oh, you precious Puritan!" she gasped, wiping her eyes. "Wow, I bet those kids were surprised!" Honestly, though, Jen, why don't you relax and get some joy out of life?" Dotty regarded Jennie thoughtfully. "You know, if you used a little more makeup and got a few sharp clothes you'd be a knockout. I wish I had your figure!"

Jennie felt relieved that her friend was not angry. She had been over this ground with several of her girlfriends, not to mention a few men, so she answered patiently, "I get a great deal of joy out of life, and I can't afford any new clothes."

"Come on, Jen, you know you'd like a man hanging around.

What woman wouldn't? You're still young. Live a little!"

Jennie knew that Dotty would never understand her philosophy on the subject. She often yearned for a husband who loved her, but the shoddy relationships she sometimes glimpsed at work did not tempt her. Sometimes at night, when everything was quiet, she viewed the long, lonely life stretching ahead with dread, but she also learned that if she kept busy there was no time for sadness. She did not want to cheapen herself and was usually able to fend off advances made by the men she met with a clever reply, or by just pretending not to hear. Another girl in the office was divorced, too, and made flippant remarks about her "ex." Jennie still felt only sadness about her own broken marriage and could not joke about it. She was brought sharply out of her reverie by Dotty's next remark.

"You know, Hon, if you would dress up and 'do the town' with me some Saturday night, I bet you'd have a dozen fellas calling you."

Jennie smiled. "You don't know what you're saying, Dotty. I would be so out of place and miserable you'd be glad to get rid of me. Besides, if the Lord *does* have a man for me, somewhere, he *won't* be in a bar, and he *will* come looking for me. I'll not go looking for him." Jennie spoke with such conviction that Dotty stared at her in amazement.

The ad appeared in the Saturday paper, and Jennie was swamped with callers. Most of them could be eliminated by a few words of conversation. The second day Jennie received a call from a girl whose Southern accent fascinated her. She made an appointment at once.

When Jennie opened the door she saw a large, rosy-cheeked young lady whose hair was very black and whose green eyes sparkled with friendliness. Jennie was captivated. "Maggie Rose," as she introduced herself, knelt by little Kathy, asking her name and telling her how pretty she was and that she had a little sister at home just her age. Kathy glowed and took Maggie into her heart at once. On guard, Jennie watched her guest carefully, but could detect only a pleasant face and sincere manner. Maggie opened her purse and offered references from former employers. Jenny asked if she had any references from former landlords.

"Ah nevah dreamed how hawd it would be to get an apahtment,

you know, so I didn't bring any references," she said apologetically. Maggie said her home was in Greensboro, North Carolina, and that until a few weeks ago she had had a very good job at home, but she had been transferred up here, which worked out very well as her fiancé was here too.

Jennie showed her the apartment and explained the arrangement. Maggie would use the foldaway bed and dressing room closet. She would also be expected to help with the housework.

Maggie exclaimed over everything, and Jennie was enchanted by her friendly manner and happy face. So they made their plans. Maggie explained that she ate downtown with Earl most evenings, as he had only a room, but she would be home on weekends. She glowed as she counted out the first month's rent.

"Mama will be so happy to know that I have a good place to stay and that there's a church nearby," she said as she placed the money in Jennie's hand.

Jennie felt more relaxed at those words and told her they would be glad to have her go to church with them. Maggie smiled. She made plans to move in Saturday afternoon, since all she had was a few personal belongings at the hotel.

The first weekend was very pleasant. Maggie was out very late on Saturday night so begged off church the next day, but she was neat and clean and cheerful, chattering on about "down home" in her fascinating drawl. She had a keen sense of humor and often brought Kathy little gifts or treats. The child accepted her wholeheartedly, and Jennie warmed to her bubbly personality. Maggie insisted on doing her part of the work, and she did it well.

She explained that she had met Earl while he was in the army stationed near her home. They had fallen in love and were to be married as soon as they could save the money. Why he was not now in the service and what he did for a living were facts that Maggie managed to avoid, and Jennie didn't feel she should inquire. Maggie said she would often be late coming in at night, but not to worry. As it turned out, she was always home by nine o'clock, full of the day's happenings and friendly as a puppy. Jennie looked forward to their talks and grew more fond of her newfound friend. Occasionally Maggie returned very late and explained that they had gone to a movie or been invited to a friend's.

One evening several weeks later Maggie came home a little less exuberant than usual. "Jennie, Honey, do you suppose I could cook supper some night and ask Earl over? He gets so tired of eating downtown."

Jennie looked up from her book. "Why, of course you may, Maggie. I'm sorry I didn't think of it myself."

The next evening Maggie came home loaded with groceries. Jennie wondered how on earth she could use all of them for one meal.

"I asked Earl to come out tomorrow evening, Jen, and I am really anxious for you to meet him." Maggie's laugh sounded a little forced. "I guess I should explain that he is not a handsome man, but I'm crazy about him," Maggie went on. "Maybe I should tell you, too, that he is older than I am and that he has been married and has two children." This was all said in a rush as though it had been planned and she wanted to get it over with. Somehow Jennie was not surprised, for she had often sensed something a little furtive in Maggie's manner when she spoke of Earl.

"How long has his wife been dead?" Jen asked matter-of-factly.

"Oh, Jennie, help me with this. I can't get the refrigerator door open!" Maggie's arms were full of things she was trying to get into the small refrigerator, and Jennie laughingly went to her rescue, not noticing that the last question had been avoided.

The next evening Maggie was already home when Jennie and Kathy came in. The apartment was spotless, the little kitchen full of tempting smells. A freshly baked pie was cooling in the kitchen window, and the small table was attractively set for four.

"I took the afternoon off so I could get dinner started," Maggie told her with her usual charming smile.

"Everything looks lovely. Can I help?" Jennie asked.

"Not yet, but Earl should be here any minute." Maggie looked around to see that everything was in place just as the front doorbell rang.

"Oh, that must be my man," she said. Jennie was surprised to see a strange look come into Maggie's eyes. Later, when thinking it over, she couldn't decide whether it was fear or apprehension. Maggie had almost looked haunted for a brief second.

Earl proved to be a stocky, dark-haired man, not quite as tall as Maggie. He was in his early or middle forties. A big black cigar hung from his sullen mouth, and he carried a folded newspaper under his arm. He grunted when Maggie introduced him. "What on earth does she see in that grouch?" Jennie wondered as she hurried Kathy into the bathroom to tidy her hair before dinner.

"Earl, Honey, if you want to wash, the bathroom is just down the hall," she heard Maggie say.

"Naw, just want to read my paper," he mumbled, and dropped into the living room chair. So far as Jennie could tell there had been no greeting between the two of them, and for an engaged couple this seemed rather strange. But she pushed the thought aside and hurried to help Maggie finish up.

"Don't mind if Earl seems cross. He's really only tired," Maggie whispered nervously.

Jennie patted her hand. "We don't mind," she said, feeling a bit sorry for Maggie, for she had never seen her so flustered.

The dinner proved that Maggie was an excellent cook, but Earl ate with no expression, wolfing down great mouthfuls. He hardly noticed Kathy or Jennie and only barked a few demands at Maggie.

"I'll be glad to clean up the dishes if you and Earl have plans for the evening," Jennie offered as Maggie was serving the pecan pie.

"Oh, would you, Jen?" Maggie shot a pleading look at Earl. "What shall we do?" she asked.

Earl filled his mouth with pie, then gulped down his coffee. "Nuttin'. Looks like rain. Think I'll go back to my room."

Maggie dropped her eyes. "Oh," she said briefly, but there was a world of chagrin in the little word. A blanket of embarrassed silence fell over the dinner table.

"Well, after such a lovely dinner it's up to me to do the dishes anyway," Jennie said at last, breaking the silence. "What a crab!" she thought to herself as she rose and began gathering up the dishes.

Maggie and Earl retreated to the living room, and after a whispered consultation, Maggie came to the kitchen and explained that they had decided to go out after all.

"Why is Maggie's friend so cross?" Kathy asked as she and Jennie put the kitchen in order. Jennie smiled at the puzzled frown creasing the child's brow.

"I don't know dear, but I'm glad Maggie isn't like that, aren't you?"

It was very late before Maggie came home that night, so they didn't talk until the next morning.

"No one knows what I see in Earl, and sometimes I wonder myself." Maggie said as the two woman sat down to munch on donuts.

Again, Jennie saw a troubled look in Maggie's usually laughing eyes. "Yes, it's true that we can't all like the same people," she said lamely, "but he is not what I would picture for you. Perhaps when I know him better I'll understand, but right now I feel that you could find someone more worthy of you."

"Oh, he can be just charming," Maggie added hastily. Jennie could see that the slightest criticism of Earl upset her friend, so she changed the subject. But she couldn't forget the almost sinister effect Earl seemed to have on Maggie.

One Saturday evening when Jennie and Kathy were invited to the Fishers, Maggie asked if she could invite Earl for dinner in their absence. Jennie was glad to be gone when he came, so gave her consent. Thereafter, Maggie entertained Earl when Jennie and Kathy were out, and it became customary for him to come on Sunday evenings while they were at church. Since they often went with a group of friends after church for refreshments, he was always gone or just leaving when they returned.

The strangest thing about the whole arrangement was Maggie's attitude, her nervous, almost apologetic air. Jennie was puzzled, but decided Maggie felt she did not like Earl, and was embarrassed.

In every other way, Maggie was a pleasant addition to their little family.

Chapter 5
The Delayed Vacation

The office where Jennie worked was a large, airy room without partitions. The desks were arranged in four neat rows with four desks each, like a large classroom. The receptionist was in the front near the door and could turn and see anyone in the office if she needed to.

One afternoon Jennie was busily transcribing letters when she was interrupted by a great deal of commotion in the front. She glanced up to see a tall, good-looking man in the uniform of a naval lieutenant, surrounded by several of the old-timers in the office. They were all laughing as he answered their noisy questions. He spoke softly, so she could not hear what he said. Just as she was turning back to her work, he raised his eyes and met hers across the large room. A shiver shot through her and left her trembling. "Why am I blushing?" she asked herself impatiently, her fingers flying over the keys. She could feel the hot blood washing over her face and throat.

"Jennie, I would like you to meet one of our former employees." Janet, the receptionist, was standing by Jennie's desk with her hand on the young officer's arm. "Mike, this is Jennie Shelby."

Jennie smiled, "Hello," she said, taking her hands off the keys and dropping them into her lap.

"I asked Janet to introduce us," Mike said. He grinned and his gray eyes seemed to see right through her. Larry had gray eyes. Jennie was confused for just a minute, and before her quick mind could come to her rescue, Janet said a quick " 'scuse me" and dashed away to answer her buzzing switchboard.

Just then Mike noticed the photograph of Kathy which Jennie

34

had framed and kept on her desk. He reached over and picked it up. "Cute girl. Your sister?"

Jennie's brows flew up like tiny black wings, and she smiled impishly. "I've heard that line before. No, she's my daughter. Now you can say, 'But you don't look old enough to have a daughter that big.' "

He grinned, and his level look seemed to penetrate her mind. "I have two little girls myself, one just about this age, and one younger." He had ignored her teasing. "My wife died two months ago, and I have been relieved of duty to come back from Germany and care for my children."

Jennie sensed a little bitterness in his tone. "I'm sorry," she said softly.

He put the picture back. "Thank you," he said, and, turning swiftly, he walked away, his back straight. It was almost as if he had clicked his heels, saluted, and marched off. "What a strange man," Jennie thought as she turned back to her typewriter.

After work that evening, when she went into the lounge to get her jacket, Dotty grabbed her arm. "What did Mike say to you? Do you know who he is?" The words tumbled excitedly out of her mouth, followed by a giggle.

"You mean Mike O'Connor?" Jennie asked, puzzled for a minute.

"Just *the* Mike O'Connor, of the velly velly exclusive O'Connors, who have been in these parts since the year one and own half the town is all!" Dotty said all in one breath. "He's about the best 'catch' in town, and sly little old Jennie is right in there pitching," she teased. "Maybe you aren't so dumb after all!"

"Honestly, Dotty!" Jennie was on the defensive at once. "You really are impossible!" Her voice was sharp as she walked out, and the door clicked shut on Dotty's rollicking laugh.

Riding home on the bus she was instantly contrite. "I wasn't very nice to her—certainly not Christlike. I must apologize tomorrow." Yet the encounter haunted her all evening.

As she and Kathy let themselves into their apartment she caught a whiff of cooking and saw Maggie coming to meet them, wiping her hands on her apron.

"I decided to come home for dinner tonight and surprise y'all," she said. Jennie felt that Maggie's usually cheerful smile was forced, and she was certain that her eyes were swollen from crying. "Poor Maggie," she thought. "I wonder if she has finally found out what a bum that Earl really is?"

As they sat down to eat, Jennie asked, "What is Earl doing tonight alone?" Maggie did not answer for a moment, and when she looked up, the naked misery in her eyes struck Jennie like a blow.

"I don't know. We had a little spat."

The two women sat talking after Kathy had gone out to play in the summer evening, lingering over the meal. Jennie told of meeting the very handsome Mike O'Connor, but sensed that Maggie was hardly listening.

"Jennie, there are some things I should tell you which I never meant to tell anyone. You have been so kind to me, and I have learned to like you more than I thought I would. Your assurance that everything can be trusted to the Lord reminds me of home and makes me feel very wicked at times. I've wanted to explain to you, but let me get out of this mess first." Maggie's eyes were downcast, and she was toying with her fork. "One thing I can tell you is that when I left home to come up here to be with Earl, it was against everything I had ever been taught. It almost broke my mother's heart. She is the kind of Christian you are." Maggie started to cry softly, and Jennie reached over and patted her hand, not knowing what to say.

"Just tell me as much as you want to, when you want to, Maggie. But I do hope you won't marry Earl until you are sure. I believe the Lord has someone much better for you."

Maggie looked up, tears streaming down her face. "I honestly do not know why he has such power over me, but when I am with him, nothing else matters, and when I am away from him—oh, you would never understand!"

"Maggie," Jennie said softly, "if you were raised in a Christian home, you know that it is wrong to even play with the idea of marrying someone not committed to Christ. We are all apt to be swayed by our emotions if we allow them to take control."

Maggie jumped up and began to gather up the dishes. "Oh, well, I'll work it out somehow. Don't worry about me."

They chatted on about unimportant things for the rest of the evening, but Jennie remembered to pray for Maggie that night before she went to bed.

The next day Maggie called Jennie at the office saying that she and Earl had patched up their quarrel and she wouldn't be home for supper. Jennie's heart sank, but she reminded herself that it was really none of her business.

Jennie's first vacation was due in August, and she and Kathy were excitedly planning their first trip to Chicago to visit her parents. They had promised to take her back to Crestview for a short visit, and Jennie felt excited about the trip. She and Kathy packed together, giggling like a couple of youngsters. The plane was scheduled to leave at 8:00 p.m., which, with a layover in Minneapolis, would put them into Chicago after 10:00—not an ideal time to be traveling with a child. But since it was the only plane they could get, Jennie decided to make the best of it.

Eileen dropped them off at the airport. They checked their baggage and found their gate. Jennie collapsed in a chair, realizing for the first time all day how really tired she was. "I've been running on pure nervous energy the past three days," she muttered. Kathy curled up in the seat beside her and was sound asleep in less than five minutes.

Jennie glanced at her watch, then looked out the window. It was 7:50, and she wondered when the airplane would pull up to the tunnel at their gate.

Just then a man came hurrying up to a group of people standing nearby. "Say, Bill, the plane's an hour late. Let's go somewhere and get a cup of coffee."

An hour late! Jennie slumped down in her chair. It would be 9:00 before they even got off the ground!

Kathy roused just then. "When's the plane coming, Mommy?" she asked in a thin voice.

"It's an hour late, Honey," Jennie replied. "We'll have to wait."

She called her parents to let them know about the delay, then held Kathy on her lap and let the child sleep with her head on her shoulder.

About five after nine an announcement came over the loudspeaker that their plane would be delayed another forty-five minutes. "Circumstances beyond our control," the announcer said in a mildly apologetic tone of voice. Audible groans went up from the waiting crowd.

Forty-five minutes later a well-dressed airline representative spoke to the passengers over the public-address system. "Your attention please, ladies and gentlemen. We regret to announce that due to fog in Minneapolis we have had to cancel tonight's flight. Any of you who live out of town may come to the desk to make hotel arrangements, which the airline will pay for. Everyone will be rescheduled for the earliest possible time."

Jennie was numb. They had waited all this time for nothing! She woke Kathy up and told her about the change of plans. Kathy began to cry. "But I want to go to Grandma's house now," she whimpered.

"Now don't cry, Honey. We'll go to Grandma's house tomorrow, but we have to get home now so you can get to bed," Jennie explained.

There was a long line at the ticket window. While Kathy dropped wearily against the overnight case, Jennifer waited . . . and waited . . . and waited. When her turn came, she was relieved to find that there was still space available on a flight the next morning, and she took the seats. She called her parents again, then made her way to the front of the terminal, where an airport limousine waited to take all passengers back to town. It was after midnight when they arrived back at the apartment.

Standing under the light by her front door, Jennie groped in her purse for her keys. Suddenly her ear caught a noise inside, an indistinct scuffling sound, followed by muted words, and then Maggie's almost hysterical voice.

"Jennie is that you?" Her southern accent left the words hanging on a high, shrill note.

Jennie was puzzled. Something was very wrong here. What was the rustling, scurrying noise?

"Jennie, please don't come in for a minute. Please wait—or use the kitchen door." Maggie's voice was choked with sobs.

All the frustrations and problems of the day seemed to engulf her, and Jennie's temper flared. Who did Maggie think she was, telling her whether she could come into her own apartment? She heard heavy footsteps in the living room, but still the light was not turned on, for there was no bright streak under the door.

"Oh Jennie, please come to the kitchen door. I will let you in." Maggie's voice was frantic, and she was sobbing. The kitchen door was only a few steps down the hall. A moment later it opened, and

Maggie, in a thin nightgown, stood just inside. Her face turned away, and she wept with great wrenching sobs. Slowly, Jennie's tired mind grasped the fact that she had walked into a very sordid situation. She marched through the kitchen into the living room just in time to see Earl leave. She looked at the tumbled bed, and the whole situation unfolded in her mind. Anger boiled up in her like a hot stream. She could hear Maggie sobbing in the kitchen, and Kathy was tugging at her skirt. "Mommy, I want to go to bed. Why is Maggie crying?"

First things first, Jennie thought grimly. She helped the weary little girl into bed and closed the bedroom door firmly.

She found Maggie a crumpled heap in the corner by the kitchen door. She was crouched on the floor, her head in her arms, crying until her whole body was trembling.

"Maggie, how could you? I trusted you, and you have been using me all the time."

Maggie raised her swollen, tear-streaked face. "You can't say anything to me that I haven't already said to myself." She choked through her tears. "I'll leave right away."

Jennie stood silent a minute, regarding the dejected lump of humanity before her. Her anger seeped away, and she remembered the Bible story of the woman taken in adultery, "in the very act." Her Lord had not condemned at that time, and certainly she should not.

"Go get a housecoat and come back. We need to talk," she said quietly.

They sat facing one another at the small dining table, Maggie's eyes a little resentful, but cautious. Jennie regarded her sadly. "What are your plans?" she asked after they had sat silently for a minute or so.

Maggie looked at her hands. She twisted a sodden handkerchief around her fingers and shrugged. A faint, wry smile curved the corners of her lips. "You spoiled any plans I had by coming home," she said softly. Then she looked up, her face sober. "I'll leave in the morning."

Jennie was growing impatient. "Don't you realize that you have jeopardized my reputation? I am accountable for the people who share my apartment." She leaned forward, "I trusted you, Maggie. You deceived me. Why?"

The tears began to roll down Maggie's face again. "I have no excuse, Jen, and I am not what you think I am. I have been Earl's mistress since before I came up here. In fact, when he came here he was leaving me, but I couldn't give him up, so I followed him. I have never done anything like this before in my life and I hate myself, but there it is."

It was hard for Jennie to grasp what Maggie had just said. "Do you mean to tell me that on Sunday nights—" her voice faltered, but Maggie caught her meaning and nodded.

"I'm sorry," she said simply.

Jennie was dazed. "If you are so much in love, why don't you get married?" she asked.

Maggie raised her head and gave Jennie a searching look. When she spoke, her voice was so low that Jennie had to bend closer to catch her words. "Because his wife won't give him a divorce. I thought you had guessed."

"Are you saying that you deliberately carried on this relationship when you knew there was no chance of marriage?"

"Yes." Maggie's voice was very tired. "He never pretended to be anything he wasn't, so I can't blame him. He told me about his marriage, his gambling, and his underworld connections—everything. He is wanted by the police down home, but I followed him anyway. Several times he has tried to break off with me, but I just couldn't give him up." She was being brutally frank, and her voice was hard.

Jennie was too tired and confused to think everything out just then, so she stood to her feet. "We have a plane to catch early in the morning, so I must get to bed," she said. "I guess you'd better move. Leave the key on the table, and let me know where you go so I can call you when I get back." She looked into Maggie's upturned face. "Honestly, Maggie, I love you very much, and this hurts me deeply. I wish I could help you. I do want you to know that I am not condemning you. Even the Lord did not condemn the woman taken in adultery, but told her to go and sin no more. He is the One you have sinned against, not me." It sounded so harsh, and she didn't want that.

Afraid to say more, Jennie turned and walked down the hall to the bedroom, her shoulders drooping with fatigue.

Chapter 6
Roger's Offer

It was not until they were finally settled on the plane the next morning that Jennie read the note she found on the dining room table when she got up.

4:00 a.m.

Dear Jennie:

I can't sleep, and I cannot face you in the morning, so I'm leaving now. Don't worry, I called the hotel and can get a room there. Right now I'm so upset that I have no plans, but you have been a good friend to me, and after I have worked this out, I will get in touch with you.

Thanks for not preaching to me. There's an old saying, and it may be in the Bible, "Be sure your sins will find you out." When I first came here, I thought I was being clever and could make you like me so much you wouldn't care what I did. My plans boomeranged on me, and as I watched you live your quiet, simple life, I began to envy your peace of mind. Believe it or not, I was that kind of person when I was younger. Then I let Earl lead me away from the Lord, and now I can't even pray. I'm too ashamed.

I must go, as my cab is waiting. Please pray for me, dear Jennie, and try not to hate me too much, for I do love you.

Maggie

41

Jennie read the note over several times as the plane sped on. She answered Kathy's excited questions absent-mindedly, for her mind was going over the months Maggie had lived with them. Poor Maggie.

In Chicago her parents greeted them eagerly. Their happy, glowing faces warmed Jennie's heart.

Later, after Kathy was in bed, Jennie told them of her various experiences. Jennie's Dad roared with laughter when she related the fiasco with the first two young roommates. "I'll bet your eyes were flashing blue fire!" he exclaimed. She decided not to mention Maggie. That incident was still too raw in her heart.

The next day they all drove to Crestview for a week. The days flashed by so fast that it was time to go home before she and Beth had time to talk. The last day they spent some time out under the big oak tree, and Jennie told her sister about Maggie and about meeting Mike O'Connor.

"Does that mean that you have finally decided you might remarry?"

"I have decided to leave it all to the Lord. If He has a husband for me somewhere, He will bring us together. I am content, and I can wait."

Beth was impatient, "You know, Jen, sometimes you just close your mind. You make me mad, and you sound so wishy-washy, so submissive! The Bible says that, 'it is not good for man to live alone!' " She paused and her anger seemed to drain away. She reached over and patted Jennie's hand. "Sorry, Honey, I just hate to see you carrying all this burden alone."

A smile hovered around Jennie's lips. "I'm fine, and I'm not alone. I just think it is better to be *willing* to obey the Lord and accept the life He permits. I have learned a lot about living by faith this year."

They flew back to Sioux City late Sunday evening.

As Jennie walked into the office on Monday morning Dotty greeted her with a welcoming grin and said she had missed her "like sixty." With a glow of pleasure Jennie settled into the familiar routine, realizing that she had sat at this desk for over a year, and it had been a very good year.

The next Friday morning Jennie was called to the phone. She picked up the receiver with a prick of apprehension. Always in the back of her mind was a dormant fear that something might happen to Kathy, but the voice on the phone was masculine and very pleasant.

"This is Roger Winter, Jennie. Hope I'm not interrupting anything."

"Oh, hello, Roger. As a matter of fact I am rather busy since I just got back from vacation, but I can spare a minute. Is Eileen all right?"

"Oh, yes, she's fine." He paused. "I wonder if you could meet me at the Green Parrot for lunch?" he asked and then he chuckled. "This is strictly business, you understand."

Jennie was curious. Roger had hardly spoken to her when they lived there, and now this. "Well, . . . I suppose I could," she began, "but I admit that you have me guessing as to what you have in mind."

He laughed heartily. "Nothing binding, just an idea I have," he said, his tone more impersonal now. "See you at noon?"

"Yes, I'll be there." She put the phone down thoughtfully.

Later, as Roger seated her at one of the small tables, she was reminded again that he was a very handsome man. "I expect you are confused by my call this morning," he said after lunch was served. "I didn't know any other way to approach you, and I think I have an offer which will be of interest to you." Jennie said nothing, so he went on. "As you know, it is difficult to find good employees these days, and I have heard that you are both good and dependable. So, frankly, I am offering you a job." His voice was now brisk and businesslike, and he looked at her intently.

"I'm very well satisfied where I am," she said quickly.

Roger raised his brows. "Wouldn't more money tempt you? And more responsibility?"

Jennie paused. "More money would be nice, particularly right now, but I would hesitate to leave Mr. Ingersoll in a mess."

Roger shrugged. "I wouldn't want you to leave without giving the proper notice, but if he can't meet my offer—and I am pretty sure he can't—then I think you would be foolish to turn it down. 'All's fair in love and war.' " His grin was boyish and charming, and Jennie was again aware that he was a very attractive man.

"What is this offer?" she asked, thinking of all the things she could do with a larger salary.

Roger explained that he needed a secretary for the sales department, and if the woman proved to be efficient, she would automatically become his private secretary when the woman who now held that job left in about three months to get married.

"I wouldn't need to get another roommate," Jennie thought. "But what if it didn't work out? I have a job now that I like."

"Well?" Roger said with just a touch of impatience.

She looked at him quickly. "Oh, I'm sorry, Roger, I was thinking about what you said. Could I have a little more time to think?" she asked.

"Of course," he replied. "We don't want you to come if you have any reservations, but I think you will be happy with us. I told Eileen this morning that I was going to ask you, and she hopes you will accept too."

The talk turned to Eileen and more personal things, so the rest of the lunch hour passed pleasantly. Jennie promised to call the next morning with her answer.

She knew what she would do before she arrived back at the office. She *did* have to think of Kathy, and the larger salary would solve so many of their problems. Kathy could have piano lessons, and they could both have much-needed new clothes. She hurried into the office, her eyes shining with excitement.

"Hey, you must have struck gold!" Dotty said, smiling. "You look all bubbly."

"You might call it that." She grinned impishly but refused to say anything more though Dotty teased and prodded all afternoon. That night she told Kathy about their fortune.

Chapter 7
The Sunday School Nightmare

After supper that evening Jennie busied herself around the kitchen, humming softly to herself. In her thoughts she was furnishing the living room, buying new clothes for them both, and dreaming about a piano. Kathy had gone out for a few minutes of play, when the doorbell rang. Jennie went happily to answer it.

Her callers were a delegation from the church: Pastor Johnson; Mr. Sullivan, superintendent of the Sunday School; and Mr. Groves, chairman of the board of deacons. Jennie greeted them warmly and invited them to sit down. They spoke of the weather and asked about her vacation.

During a lull in the conversation Jennie noticed Mr. Sullivan watching her. He was a small shrimp of a man, she thought with eyes like a snake. Sitting forward in his chair, he twirled his hat on his forefinger.

"Mrs. Shelby," he rasped, "we have a rather unpleasant duty to perform tonight, and we may as well get it over with." His glance darted to the other men, and Jennie's heart plunged. Both Pastor Johnson and Mr. Groves watched him, refusing to look at her. Mr. Sullivan cleared his throat nervously and continued.

"We have just come from a meeting of the Sunday School board, and it was decided that, in view of the fact that you are a divorced woman, it is best to ask someone else to take over your class."

Jennie was stunned. Her mind raced, and her mouth was dry. She loved every girl in that class. She had put her whole self into being a good teacher. What did being divorced have to do with her desire to serve the Lord? Was she a second-class Christian because her husband had deserted her for another woman? Didn't it make any difference *why* she was divorced? Anger flashed through her nerves clear to her fingertips, but she realized that Mr. Sullivan was still talking.

"Please understand that we have investigated you, and everyone speaks well of you. You do live an exemplary life." He clicked his false teeth and cleared his throat. "However, we feel that it is not a good example for our young people for a woman with your past to stand before these sweet young girls as an example."

Mr. Groves, a weak, but well-meaning man interrupted in a conciliatory tone. "We do hope you understand our position, Mrs. Shelby. We wouldn't hurt you for the world, but we do have our young folks to think about." He seemed unable to meet Jennie's level look, for her eyes flashed the deep hurt and anger she felt.

Pastor Johnson, a young and inexperienced man, was clearly distressed. "Mrs. Shelby," he said quietly, "I want you to know that I, as your pastor, do not agree with Mr. Sullivan. But after the board made its decision, I had no choice but to cooperate. We know that you are a sincere and earnest Christian." He coughed. "We even checked with your former pastor, who wrote saying he could not praise you highly enough and that you were without blame in the breakup of your marriage, but well, ah, some folks cannot overlook the fact that divorce is involved."

Jennie blessed him silently for his obvious concern, but anger washed over her and she spoke sharply. "I think this is all very unfair, and I resent being 'investigated' like a common criminal." She sat very straight and looked pointedly at Mr. Sullivan, who was engrossed with his hat.

"Why didn't you ask me, if you wanted to know about my 'past' as you call it? If you knew how much I hate divorce, the shame of it, the waste of it—" Her voice caught. "I am a *good* teacher, and believe me, I can help others better because of my heartache than one who has not suffered." She blinked back the tears. A little part of her chided, "Jennie, you are being nasty." Aloud she said, "I'm sorry, I don't intend to be unreasonable, but it really hurts."

Pastor Johnson spoke again. "We must be going, Mrs. Shelby. I do hope our visit has not caused you more pain. I personally feel it is a shame to allow one with your talent to sit idle, but I am only one voice," he said weakly, but his handshake was sincere.

"Oh, by the way," Mr. Sullivan said as they were leaving, "my daughter will take the class next Sunday, so you will be spared an explanation to the class."

Jennie bit her lip. Anger was boiling up in her again, so she just nodded her head as they all said goodnight.

"What was that about?" Kathy asked as she came in the back door.

"Oh, nothing." Jennie couldn't explain, for she had always tried to protect Kathy from the feeling of rejection she often felt. "They just came to call, and I've decided not to teach for a while."

"Oh," Kathy said vaguely. She seemed puzzled, for she knew how her mother enjoyed her class, but said no more.

After Kathy was in bed and the apartment quiet, Jennie dropped to her knees and sobbed a prayer, asking the Lord for more understanding and compassion. She knew she must be willing to forgive Mr. Sullivan, but not quite yet.

Later she fell into bed exhausted, but it was some time before she fell asleep. When she did, she drifted into a haunting dream. She seemed to be hurrying through a dark woods and the trees swayed around her. She was running from some terrible danger, petrified with fear, when suddenly she saw a light at the end of the narrow path. But almost at once she saw a huge snake coiled in the way, writhing and turning its head. She fell back in horror. Its face was Mr. Sullivan's, but he was weeping, his eyes pleaded, and great tears streamed down his face. She turned to run, but couldn't move, nor could she scream. She woke up fighting the covers and sweating with fear. What a relief to awake to a cool, dark summer night, with moonbeams dancing on the ceiling and Kathy sleeping peacefully in a bed near hers. She breathed a prayer of thanksgiving that it was only a dream.

She got up and slipped out to the kitchen for a glass of milk, then went to bed again, this time to sleep, deep and sweet.

Chapter 8
Mike O'Connor

The next morning Jennie lay for a long time going over in her mind the previous evening's disturbing scene and the haunting dream it had caused. She could not forget the torment in the eyes of the snake with Mr. Sullivan's face. "It's much easier to forgive than to forget," she thought. "I must forgive him. If I hadn't wanted to do this teaching so much to honor the Lord, it wouldn't be so hard. It makes me feel soiled."

She was still wrestling with these thoughts when she suddenly remembered that today was the day she was to call Roger about the job. Since it was Saturday, she called him at home, and she felt better after a conversation with both Roger and Eileen. "At least they don't feel I'm an outcast," she thought rebelliously. They had invited her to bring Kathy and come for dinner on Sunday evening. Ordinarily she would have declined, since she always reserved that time for her evening church service, but she decided to skip church this time.

On Sunday morning she sent Kathy to Sunday School alone. When Kathy questioned her about it, she dismissed it by reminding her that she wouldn't be teaching for a while.

The visit with Roger and Eileen was very pleasant, yet Jennie sensed a strangeness between herself and Eileen. It was not so much that Eileen was unfriendly, but that Roger was so much more friendly. There was a look in Eileen's eyes, as though she wanted to say something, but hesitated. However, overall she had a nice time, and Roger drove them home in his big car so that they didn't have to ride the bus.

Jennie handed in her resignation the Monday following her

visit with Roger and Eileen. She was a little puzzled at Mr. Ingersoll's strange smile, but he accepted her resignation with no comment. The next two weeks passed quickly.

Several of the girls in the office planned a fairwell dinner for her on her last Friday evening and then proposed that everyone walk over to the nearby bowling alley to watch the company team play. It sounded like fun to Jennie, who had been unable to afford any recreation for so long.

Jennie had bought a new suit for the occasion. "You look pretty snazzy tonight," Dotty said with a sly smile. "I knew you could do it!"

The bowling alley was hazy with smoke. The air stung Jennie's eyes and throat. "I'm a little out of place here," she thought.

"Oh, look who's playing over there!" Dotty whispered. "I didn't know he was on our team."

Jennie's eyes followed her friend's pointing finger. "Who is it?" she asked.

Dotty chuckled. "Don't you know? It's your friend, Mike O'Connor. He is managing one of our branches now, but I didn't know he was on the bowling team."

Out of uniform Mike looked very different. The heavy air, the strangeness, and loud voices whirled through Jennie's brain, leaving her a little dizzy.

"Hello, again," a strange voice said, and Jennie looked up into Mike's piercing gray eyes.

Quick as a wink there was the swish of a skirt, and Dotty said, "Hi, Mike. Here, take my seat. I want to see someone over there," and she was gone.

Mike winked at Jennie and took the empty seat. "What's this I hear about your leaving the company?" he asked, his eyes regarding her intently.

"I had a better offer," she explained.

"Yeah, good ol' Rog, always did pride himself on having the best," he laughed.

Jennie noticed a strange reflection in his voice and looked at him with a puzzled expression. So often she noticed the same reaction when Roger's name was mentioned. What did it mean? "Do you know Roger?" she asked.

He nodded. "Known him for years. We belong to the same country club, play golf together, that kind of thing." They sat silent watching the players for a few minutes.

"By the way," he asked, turning to look at her, "are you listed in the phone book? I've thought of calling you several times, but just never did."

Jennie's heart pounded, "Yes, I am," she replied quietly.

"I'll be glad to drop you at home, if you don't have a way planned," he said just before he left to go back to the game.

"Thank you, but I came on the bus with three other girls, and I probably should go back with them."

"Why don't I just take all of you?" he suggested. "I'm in no hurry."

Jennie smiled. "That would be nice. I'm sure they would prefer a car to the bus. Thank you very much."

Mike excused himself to go back to play. Jennie told Dotty about his offer when she came back.

"Velly, velly nice," Dotty crowed. Jennie wished she weren't so flippant, but that was just Dotty.

After he had dropped the other girls off at their homes, Mike drove around and showed Jennie some of the city she had not seen.

"I think I should go home now," she said presently. "I don't like to break up this pleasant evening, but I left my little girl with the lady across the hall, and I don't want to keep her up too late."

"You are quite the little mother, aren't you?" he joked.

"No, not really, but being mother and father is rather time consuming, you know," she said defensively.

For the first time since she was a little girl, Jennie began to neglect her personal devotional time. She avoided Sunday School, though she sent Kathy faithfully, and nearly always attended the worship service herself. But Sunday evenings found her with Mike and the children, picnicking, horseback riding, or swimming at the country club. To be introduced as "Mike's girl" was a sweet experience. She was able to close her eyes and ears to a few sordid incidents, like the time she surprised a couple in a burning embrace behind some shrubbery near the swimming pool or when someone got disgustingly drunk. She shrugged, and reasoned that these things could happen anywhere.

The pleasant fall days gradually deepened into winter, and

Jenny found herself spending more and more time alone with Mike. Jennie's bubbling brought a twinkle to Mike's eyes, and he often sat watching her lazily as he drew on his pipe. Sometimes he teased her about "talking with her hands" and held them clasped in his, but they always dissolved in laughter when he saw that she really needed them to express herself.

Jennie adjusted to her new job easily and quickly became acquainted with the girls in the office. Roger was friendly and often stopped at her desk to chat or make some remark about the time when she would move to the desk in his outer office. She had anticipated some jealousy on the part of the other girls but felt none and decided that they knew she had been hired for the position. Roger's secretary left in November and Jennie took over the new responsibilities.

Mike had a full-time housekeeper, so he had no baby-sitting problems, and Jennie worked out an arrangement with Mrs. Carpenter to come across the hall and sit with Kathy two or three evenings a week. Every evening Mike picked her up at the office and drove her home, for which she took a lot of teasing, but she loved it. He was so handsome, so tall and graceful with his light-brown, curly hair and piercing gray eyes! Much of his charm lay in his slow smile, which began back of his eyes and spread to his whole face, revealing a fetching dimple in one cheek. Jennie's heart always turned over as she walked out to meet him after work.

Mike was open with her about everything except his dead wife, and, although he asked many questions about her past, he never mentioned his own and became quiet and withdrawn anytime she brought it up. This left Jennie puzzled at times. Mike had never even attempted to kiss her good night. At first she had worried about this and dreaded each date a little, wondering how she would handle the situation when it finally came. She didn't feel as close to the Lord as she used to and couldn't pray about it as she would have before.

But she relaxed as the weeks drifted into months for he was still the same and made no attempt to caress her, except with his eyes. In fact, at times she even felt a little piqued, wondering if there was some lack in her, and wishing he would be a little more ardent.

She kept reminding herself that she must not become really emotionally involved with someone who made no pretense of being a Christian. Somehow she never found quite the right occasion to talk to Mike about her relationship with Christ. So they drifted, and the days swept by.

Sometimes when she left Kathy in the evening, Jennie's heart smote her. She sensed the yearning in the child's eyes and in her lingering embrace, but Kathy never uttered a word of complaint. "I must spend more time with her," Jennie thought, but the days were so full. Once in a while, after she was in bed, she would think longingly of the time when her life had been less complicated, but she excused herself with the thought that the people at church had turned away from her because she was divorced, and now she had many friends who didn't mind. The still small voice in her heart chided her, but she turned a deaf ear. Soon the tormenting little voice spoke less and less.

Jennie's parents came for Christmas that year, but Jennie seemed only partly aware of their presence. She enjoyed the excited chatter, the news from home, and the remarks when she showed them all the new things she had been able to buy for the apartment, but part of her mind was always thinking of Mike and wondering if he was thinking of her. She didn't mention him to her parents. Somehow she couldn't. After all, he had never given her any reason to feel that they were more than friends, and she must wait for him to speak.

Just before they left, Jennie's mother told her that her cousin, Paul Gobel, had written for her address, saying that he was opening a pediatric clinic in Oak Park, Illinois, and might have a job if Jennie was interested.

"I wish you were closer to home," Her mother said wistfully.

"But we're just getting settled here," Jennie said. "It would be nice to be closer, though. Time will tell."

Chapter 9
The New Year's Party

A blizzard warning on Christmas day caused Jennie's parents to hasten their departure. Jennie was almost glad to be alone again. Mike was still out of town, so she went to work each morning and came home at night on the bus. As the evenings passed she began to wait nervously for his call. They had plans to go to the New Year's Eve party at the country club, and she needed to talk to him about it. After listening to some of the remarks about former New Year's Eve parties, she began to wish she hadn't promised to go. "I wish he would go with me to the Watch Night service at the church," she thought, but she knew he would only laugh at her if she mentioned it. Something told her that she was out of her depth, but she refused to listen.

When the phone finally rang, she ran to answer it, her hand trembling and her heart hammering. Mike talked casually for a few minutes, mentioning that they had been back in town several days but he had been busy. Jennie felt chagrined as she realized how eager she had been to hear from him. Evidently it had not been as important to him. He mentioned the New Year's Eve party, and she fell right in with his plans, asking how to dress and when he would pick her up.

"I'll be ready." Her eyes were a little wistful as she turned away from the phone. She didn't like herself very much these days.

She decided to wear her new dress. It was made of soft-blue taffeta, cut on good lines, with a slim waist and wide, flaring skirt. The sweetheart neckline was a little low and outlined with rows of tiny white sequins. It was a bit daring for her usual needs, but very flattering. She had felt very reckless when she bought it. She preened herself in front of the mirror, wondering if it was too flashy. Kathy watched her dress, eyes glowing with adoration, and said that her mother looked like a fairy queen.

"You'll be the prettiest of all, Mother," she remarked.

"Thank you, Honey, but I'd almost rather be at home with you."

Kathy was puzzled. "Would you *really?* Why?"

"Oh, I don't know. I just don't feel quite right about this party," she replied vaguely.

Mike whistled when she opened the door to greet him. "You look lovely, tonight, Chum," he grinned. He looked pretty nice himself, Jennie thought, and she told him so. She had always felt he was almost too handsome for his own good. He was the only son of very wealthy parents and inclined to arrogance, but his manner with her had been above reproach.

They planned to have dinner at the club with Roger and Eileen before the party began, and this was one excuse Jennie gave herself for going. She somehow felt that she was getting in too deep, but if Eileen was there everything should be all right.

Eileen wore a beautiful black chiffon which must have cost three times the price of Jennie's dress and looked it. It brought out the exquisite color in her flawless skin and golden mass of hair, but her eyes held such deep sadness that Jennie wondered if something was terribly wrong.

"Eileen, don't you feel well?" she asked when they were alone for a few minutes.

"I'm all right. Why?" she said. She sounded bored.

"I don't know, I just thought you looked sad or troubled." Jennie was a little embarrassed. Many years ago, there was nothing she could not have discussed with Eileen, but now there was a strange wall between them. Eileen drew in her breath quickly, as though she was about to confide something, then seemed to reconsider, and her voice was harsh when she spoke.

"I don't like these parties. Roger always drinks too much, and it embarrasses me. But it's good business and he is very popular." She laughed bitterly. "I guess I don't need to tell you since you're his secretary." She turned away. Jennie felt hurt. Was her old friend jealous? Eileen had always been so open and generous. It hurt to have her change.

Jennie noticed with dismay that all three of her dinner partners were starting with cocktails. She sat in thoughtful silence, listening to their chatter, until the meal was served.

"Come on, Jennie, aren't you going to have even one drink?" Roger chided with a frown.

Before she could answer Mike spoke up. "Let her alone, Rog. She doesn't drink and she doesn't smoke, and I like her that way."

Roger gave him a level look and shrugged. "Well, that figures."

"What did he mean?" Jennie wondered. Roger was a strange man. Even at the office he was either almost too personal or brisk and businesslike.

Dancing began as the evening wore on. They all knew she didn't dance, so Eileen whirled away in Roger's arms for a brief dance but was soon back with Jennie. Several of the others did not dance, so the tables were not all empty.

It was not that Jennie didn't want to dance, but she had not been allowed to learn as a girl. Now she felt embarrassed and awkward. She loved good music, and had always enjoyed watching the swirl and dip of the old dances, but this twisting and jerking only looked to her like it would be very tiresome.

As time passed, she realized that both Roger and Mike were drinking too much. Both spoke with thickened tongues, and Roger's eyes were bloodshot and bleary. Eileen had only had the one cocktail before dinner and sat sullenly beside Jennie, saying very little, her fingers nervously toying with the stem of her water glass. Suddenly she turned and looked Jennie squarely in the eyes. "Jen, you are a real disappointment to me," she said bluntly. "I always thought if anyone was steady and dependable, you were that person. I never dreamed that I would be at one of these 'rat races' with *you.*" Her eyes were angry.

A wave of self-loathing swept over Jennie, and she dropped her eyes. "I don't belong here, Eileen, and I feel very out of place," she said softly.

Eileen looked away. "You aren't serious about Mike, are you?" she asked.

Jennie's heart turned over. "Am I?" she wondered, but aloud she said, "I really don't know, but I'm not comfortable about the situation."

Eileen leaned toward her, and in her eyes there was just a glimpse of the old Eileen, the friend she had loved years ago.

"Don't, Jennie. Don't cheapen yourself. He's not for you. Do you know how his wife died?"

Jennie caught her breath. "No, I don't. He never talks about it."

Eileen went on in a rush of words. "She was an alcoholic, and one day in a drunken stupor she shot herself. They had just had a violent quarrel, and he had walked out." Eileen lifted her glass and took a sip of water. "She and Mike used to drink constantly. They met at college and went out together a few times, always drinking. One night she told Mike she was pregnant, and they went out and got married while they were both smashed."

Eileen leaned closer and put her hand on Jennie's arm. "I have to tell you this, even if it upsets you, Jen. She was always in and out of hospitals, taking 'the cure,' but it never worked." She sighed. "Mike came home that day and found her dead. Fortunately, the maid had taken the children to the park, so they were spared the ghastly sight." Eileen straightened. "Mike changed after that and stopped drinking entirely. Everyone thought he had been cured, until tonight."

Eileen sipped her water again. Jennie watched her in a daze. "He's a spoiled and selfish man, Jen. Don't throw yourself away. Everyone who knows him is watching with interest, for we do not think his intentions are honorable. He'd never marry anyone with your background. An affair, yes. Marriage, no. Don't fall for his line, Jennie."

Jennie sat speechless as Eileen finished talking. She didn't know what to say, so she said nothing, but her mind was reeling.

Mike and Roger swayed back to the table, laughing coarsely and slapping one another on the back. The orchestra broke into "Auld Lang Syne." "Happy New Year!" everyone shouted.

Suddenly Mike reached over and grabbed Jennie. Pulling her into his arms, he kissed her soundly on the lips, almost upsetting her chair. His kiss was wet and smelled of liquor. A feeling of such deep loathing swept over Jennie that she almost slapped him. And this was the kiss she had thought about, yearned for many times during the past months!

"Dear Lord, forgive me," she breathed, hardly realizing what she had said. It seemed that everyone was kissing everyone else. Jennie straightened her chair and wiped her mouth with her handkerchief, but that rancid taste and smell of the liquor clung to her lips. Mike was wandering among the tables, catching and kissing every woman who got in his way.

While she watched, Jennie's thoughts flew to her little church where she knew many friends were gathered for fellowship and prayer as they welcomed in another year. "Oh, I wish I were there!" she thought.

Soon after midnight, the crowd began to break up with much laughing and shouting. Most people were making plans to meet some other place, but Jennie held firmly to her decision to go home.

"The night's still young," Mike muttered thickly.

She was afraid of this tall, swaggering stranger with glazed eyes and blurred speech.

"You're free to go any place you like after you take me home," Jennie insisted. As soon as she said the words she realized that she must have sounded quite upset.

"Oh, aw-right," he said angrily.

Jennie also realized that in his foggy mind he felt she was angry at him. He could not understand that her anger was directed at her own weakness.

They were surprised to find about six inches of new snow on the ground when they left the clubhouse. There was much calling back and forth, with people teasing each other about driving carefully so that there would be no arrests.

The words rang out in the cold night air. "Arrest!"

How could she ever explain to her friends and to Kathy, if Mike should be arrested? "Oh, Lord, please just get me out of this mess, and I'll be more careful next time," she breathed.

She sat stiffly as they made their way to her home through the snow-clogged streets. The snowplows were busy, and there was a lot of traffic, but Mike drove silently and very cautiously, realizing that he was not at his best. The cold air seemed to clear his mind, and they arrived at the apartment with no incidents. Jennie had sat all the way without speaking, immersed in her own thoughts.

When they pulled up in front of the apartment he turned a little in the seat to face her, leaving the motor running. "Jennie, I'm afraid you didn't have much fun tonight." His voice sounded perfectly sober now.

She could not lie about it, so smiled and said, "It was a new experience for me, I must admit."

He reached over and took her hands in his. "Jennie, during the last few months we have talked about nearly everything except one. It wasn't because I haven't thought of it, but I am a cautious man, and I wanted to get to know you a little better. I admire your mind and your clean living, but how do you feel about sex? You have a beautiful body. Surely you have faced this question before?"

Jennie could hardly believe she had heard correctly. At first she felt like laughing, but his eyes were very serious. She pulled her hands away and looked at him, her eyes enormous with surprise, but no words came. She couldn't think how to answer him.

"I mean it," he said calmly. "I have been patient, but there comes a time to 'pay the piper.' "

Jennie dropped her eyes to her hands that were folded in her lap. Her mind reeled. It seemed like a terrible nightmare. Suddenly a calmness enveloped her, and she heard herself speaking. "I understand what you mean, and I suppose you feel you deserve an answer, although I am still old-fashioned enough to feel that there are some things too private for discussion. I do *not* think sex is a dirty word. It is a very special, God-given way for married people to express their love for one another." She paused. "The sickening thing to me is the way it is discussed, joked about, and cheapened these days. The sins of adultery and fornication are strongly condemned in the Bible. Did you know that?"

She felt a boldness she hadn't believed possible. Mike dropped his eyes before she went on.

"I would never be able to have an affair with you, if that is your question," she finished bluntly.

Mike shrugged his shoulders. "Well, I asked, and you answered," he said curtly. He got out of the car and came around to help her. Remarking that the snow was pretty deep and her slippers frail, he stopped and lifted her slight form in his arms, intending to carry her to the door. Turning, he slipped and fell, landing them both in a drift of the soft, newly fallen snow. It all happened so quickly that Jennie hardly realized what had happened until she found herself sprawled in the snow and Mike floundering at her side. The humor of the situation hit her at once, and she started to laugh. Mike looked at her in stunned relief, and his booming laugh joined hers. Peal after peal of laughter rang out in the winter night. Suddenly she realized what a racket they were making, and her hand flew up to cover her mouth.

Mike helped her to her feet, and she brushed off the snow. He took her key and opened the door for her, as he had always done. However, tonight he tried to push his way into the apartment rather than bidding her good night at the door.

"Please, Mike. I'm very tired and it's late. I'd really rather you didn't come in tonight."

"Are you angry?" he asked.

"No, not really, but I don't want to talk anymore. Please go." To her relief, he turned, and the last she saw of him he was groping his way into his car, whistling.

The babysitter had fallen asleep on the couch, but since she lived in the building it was no problem to rouse her and send her on her way. Jennie spoke sharply with her, and she felt ashamed at the surprised and hurt look on the girls' face as she left.

Alone, Jennie dropped into a chair, her head spinning and her thoughts confused. "You have no one to blame but yourself, young lady," she scolded herself. "You knew better than to encourage this relationship. If only Mike hadn't been so disgusting tonight. I hate what liquor does to people!" She rubbed her forehead with her hand. "I've probably spoiled my friendship with Eileen too."

Jennie's thoughts chased themselves round and round, but still she couldn't pray. She pulled herself out of her chair and began to undress, vowing that the very next day she would think everything through and decide what to do next.

Chapter 10
A New Year, A New Life

Jennie was awakened the next morning by a childish voice and tousled head burrowing into her shoulder. "Wake up, Mommy. Why are you crying?"

Jennie looked into the wide blue eyes gazing at her, eyes that adored and trusted her, and her heart throbbed with pain. "Was I crying, Honey? I must have been dreaming." She cuddled the soft form close. "It couldn't have been very bad, since I can't even remember it," she said, kissing the top of the child's head.

"I like to come into your bed, Mommy," Kathy said with one of her quick changes of mood.

"M-m-m, and I like to have you," Jennie said, hugging her tightly. "What a big girl you are getting to be! Pretty soon you will be as tall as your mother."

"I want to be just like you," Kathy said.

Jennie choked. "What a wicked, selfish woman I've been," she scolded herself.

Kathy jumped up and tugged at Jennie's hand. "I'm hungry, Mommy."

"Then we'd better get up and see what we can find to eat. Let's have a special treat this morning. I'll make hot cakes!"

They prepared breakfast together happily, and a holiday spirit filled the little kitchen.

"Since this is New Year's Day we should plan something special to do," Jennie suggested.

Kathy's eyes glowed. "Why not go sledding? There's lots of snow!"

"We'll see. I really don't have anything to wear for that, but maybe we can rig up something." Jennie rose from the table and began to gather up the dishes. Just then the phone rang. Her heart sank, "Oh, don't let it be Mike," she prayed silently. "I'm not ready for that yet."

The call was for Kathy. Mrs. Braun, her Sunday School teacher, lived on a large farm and was inviting the class for a tobaggoning party. Kathy turned to her mother. "Oh, Mother, may I go?" Her voice was excited. "It will be such fun!"

Jennie's heart sank. She had looked forward to spending the day with her daughter, but a small voice reminded her that Kathy had never interfered with her plans.

"Yes, of course you may."

Kathy hurriedly made the arrangements, telling them where to pick her up, and asking when to be ready. She had scarcely hung up the phone, though, when her face fell. "I didn't think, Mother, that you'll be alone." Kathy's eyes were sad. "I think I'll call back and tell them I can't go."

Jennie put her arms around the child. "You'll do no such thing. I will be fine, and you'll be back before dinner. There are several things I need to do here anyway. Besides, I'm tired. I'd like to just stay at home today."

Kathy's excitement began to build again. "Honest? You don't mind?" Kathy asked, searching her mother's face.

"Cross my heart. And Kathy, I love you very much for being so thoughtful." She gave the girl an extra squeeze. "Now we'd better get you ready. I would like you to make the beds before you dress, if you have time. I must clean the kitchen," she said briskly.

Kathy scurried away to do as she was told, and Jennie began to put things in order in the kitchen.

Kathy left in a flurry of welcome squeals from the children already in the car. Jennie dressed slowly and made plans for preparing dinner later on. She decided that in the meantime she would try to catch up on her letters.

Arranging her writing material on the small dining table, she sat down, but found she could think of nothing to say nor any way to begin. Scenes flashed across her mind that reminded her of the thoughtless and selfish life she had adopted. "I have really neglected Kathy," she admitted. "Poor child, left two and three nights each week with strangers while her mother acted like a silly schoolgirl. And I let it happen because I felt mistreated at church!" She dropped her head into her arms, and with no effort began to pray as the sobs welled up in her throat.

"Lord, help me. I can't stand myself. Please forgive me for being so selfish and for leaving Kathy so much." For the first time for almost a year, Jennie felt that her prayer was being heard, and she pleaded for forgiveness and guidance. "I know I have been a poor example of a Christian. I want to feel Your presence in my life again."

She wept and prayed alternately for a long time. Her mind searched the past months, and she freely laid before the Lord her own disobedience. She thought of Maggie and realized that she had come perilously near to making the same mistake. "Oh, Father, how can You love me? I know You do, but I don't deserve it."

By now Jennie was weeping and praying out loud. She dropped from her chair to her knees and bent with her face almost touching the floor. "Oh, God, please protect me from myself. I want more than anything in the world to do Your will, and if that includes a husband, thank You; but if it doesn't, just give me the grace to accept that too."

She finally raised her head and stood to her feet. Her eyes were swollen from tears, but her heart was light, for at last she felt again the sweet communion between herself and God. She knew that she must break up with Mike at once, and she must return to church and make a few apologies. She had not always been gracious to those who had hurt her. "Thank You, Lord," she said softly as she went into the living room to get her Bible.

For the first time in her life, Jennie had to dust the Book before she opened it. Once more, she bowed her head and said a brief prayer for guidance. Even before she had finished the prayer, the Bible fell open in her hands and when she looked down a verse stood out, almost as though it had been written in letters of fire. As she read, she seemed to hear a voice in the room that read to her: "Fear not; for thou shalt now be ashamed: neither be thou confounded; for thou shalt not be put to shame: for thou shalt forget the shame of thy youth, and shall not remember the reproach of thy widowhood any more."

Jennie gasped and read the passage over several times, glancing to see where it was found. "Isaiah 54:4," she murmured aloud.

"Why, that was written just for me. My widowhood is a reproach, the shame of my youth! Oh, thank You, Lord." Her voice was low and fervant. "I will remember this promise forever, for now I know that in Your time and in your own way you will remove this shameful widowhood from me."

She read on quietly, her heart almost bursting. "The Lord hath called thee as a woman forsaken and grieved in spirit, and a wife of youth, when thou wast refused, saith thy God. For a small moment have I forsaken thee; but with great mercies will I gather thee." Isaiah 54:6, 7.

"It *is* just for me," she marveled. "I claim this promise, Lord. Don't let me forget it, no matter how discouraged I may become."

She sat awhile, amazed at the miracle of prayer and the grand promise contained in the verses she had just read. Her heart was at peace, and she realized that at last she was hungry again for God.

When she finally rose, she glanced at the clock and was surprised to discover that it was well past noon. She would have to hurry to get supper started.

She quickly stirred up a small loaf and popped it into the oven. Then she prepared a sandwich and glass of milk for herself. She felt light as a feather, almost too happy to eat. A song bubbled in her throat and she found herself whistling: "My hope is built on nothing less Than Jesus' blood and righteousness. . . ."

Oh, how good to feel right again! It was almost like a joyous homecoming. She felt brave and sure, and her feet hardly touched the floor as she moved around the little kitchen.

Kathy came home in a rush of cold air, her clothes covered with snow and her cheeks glowing like red apples. Jennie grabbed her, hugging and kissing her fiercely. Kathy's blue eyes questioned her as she took off her wet things, but Jennie only smiled and asked, "Did you have a nice time, Honey?"

"Oh, yes!" Kathy giggled. "They have the nicest big dog, and he went with us." Her eyes sparkled. "He romped and played with us and rolled in the snow. He was so funny!" She held her hands apart to show how big the animal was: "So-o-o big—like the Eskimos have."

"You mean a Husky?" Jennie asked. "They make wonderful family dogs."

"I wish I had a dog, Mother, but I guess we can't in an apartment, huh?" Kathy sounded wistful.

"No, I'm afraid not," Jennie agreed, and she mentally chalked up another disadvantage to their way of living. "Lord, help me to make it up to her. She's blameless."

It was a festive evening. After dinner they played Scrabble, and Kathy's bright sense of humor kept them laughing. They finished the evening with hot chocolate and cookies, agreeing that it had been a very special day indeed.

Chapter 11
An Affair?

At the office the next day, Jennie slipped quickly into the familiar routine. The experience of New Year's Day had shaken her to her roots, but today she felt cleansed and strong. She promised herself that when Mike called she would be polite and cool, and taper off their friendship. Mike's way of life was completely foreign to hers, and she wanted to live differently. He would probably classify her as a fanatic, but she could accept that.

Roger did not come in until almost noon. His greeting was very curt as he went into his office and she knew from experience to wait until he called her. He usually stopped at her desk for a pleasant chat and then expected her to follow him into his office with a rundown on any calls or important appointments before she took his daily dictation. Most of the time he was a very kind, considerate man to work for, but lately his spells of irritability had increased, and he seemed to need more time to adjust before he faced the day. Jennie had decided it must be something personal. The business was expanding and prospering. She saw no problem there. Her feminine intuition prompted her to let him work it out, even though she felt once or twice that he had been on the verge of discussing something with her. Perhaps it had to do with Eileen, and knowing her loyalty to her old friend, he did not feel free to speak about it.

In a few minutes she heard his voice on the intercom asking her to come in. She picked up her pad and pencils and the mail which needed his attention and entered his office.

"You look better than I feel this morning," he said gruffly.

Jennie noticed that his eyes were bloodshot, and he looked

65

drawn and tired. She could not honestly tell him that he looked well, so she said, "Thank you, I never felt better," and launched into the day's business. He followed her lead, and they became involved in several items that needed his attention. His dictation took only about forty-five minutes, but when she rose to go back to her desk, he said, "Wait, Jennie, I want to talk to you."

"Oh?" she sank quietly back into her chair, her hands folded in her lap.

"You are never still a minute, are you?" he grunted. "What's the situation between you and Mike?"

Jennie's dark brows flew up. He had never been that personal before, and she resented it.

"Oh, I know it's none of my business," he growled, "but I am interested in all my employees. And I need you, Jennie."

Jennie dropped her eyes to the floor and said, "You need not worry about my leaving this job. I need it as much as you need me, Roger."

Roger cleared his throat and said in a low voice, "You did not answer my question."

Jennie could feel the scarlet color washing up into her cheeks as she replied. "Mike and I are just good friends. Why?"

"Good!" Roger's voice became more impersonal as he stood up. "I'm having lunch at the club and will play bridge before I go to the board meeting. What time is my appointment with Wiley?"

She rose, too, giving him the information he wanted, grateful not to have to talk any more about her private life. What did he know that she didn't? He and Mike were friendly. Had they discussed her? Having been hurt all those years ago by Larry, she always found it a bit difficult to really trust a man.

The work at hand soon absorbed Jennie's attention, and it was not until she was clearing her desk, preparing to go home, that she remembered that Mike had not called. A slight disappointment crossed her mind for a moment, but she knew it was better this way.

Back at the apartment, Kathy was full of chatter about her day's activities. Jennie listened with half her mind as she prepared the evening meal. The phone rang just as they were finishing the dishes. To her relief, it was only one of Kathy's friends.

The evening wore on. The much-awaited call came after Kathy

was in bed, just as Jennie was preparing her grocery list for the next day's shopping.

Mike's greeting was very casual, and he made no effort to explain where he had been or what he had been doing. "Are you all right?" he asked.

"Why yes, I'm fine." Jennie was puzzled. "Why?"

"I'm ashamed to say it, but I don't remember much that happened after we left the club," he replied. "I just wanted to be sure I was a gentleman."

"You were fine."

The talk turned to the weather and the latest news, and then Mike said, "good night," and, "see ya," and was gone.

As Jennie put the phone down, she realized that this was the first time for several months that he had not made plans for their next meeting before saying good night. She smiled wryly. "Thank You, Lord, I guess You are protecting me from myself."

The weeks moved slowly by, and Jennie and Kathy slipped into a very pleasant routine, enjoying one another more and more. Kathy was ten years old now and very good company. Jennie found her work most absorbing, and she became more and more involved at the office. Roger was kind—almost too solicitous at times—and he gave her more and more responsibility. Her salary also grew, so that it was possible for them to have a few luxuries. But as Kathy grew, so did the needs, and it seemed that there was always something just out of reach. Yet life was very good.

Bob and Beth came for Thanksgiving that year, and the reunion was sweet. Then came the bustle and gaity of the holidays, and another year gone.

The following year the company received a very large order that made it necessary for Jennie to work extra hours. Roger offered to take her to dinner each time he asked her to stay, but she preferred to get a sandwich at the corner drugstore. But one day he called her into the office and remarked, "Jennie, I'm afraid I'll have to stay a couple of hours tonight. Why not let me take you to dinner first?"

Jennie felt apologetic about always refusing. "I really appreciate your offer, Roger, but honestly, I'd rather just dash into the drugstore. It's much faster. I know that Kathy is getting to be a big girl, and I know that Mrs. Carpenter is right across the hall, but still I don't like to leave her any more than is necessary."

His smile was tight. "You act like you think I might bite," he grunted.

"No, it isn't that at all," she replied.

"All right," he said, brightening, "I'll go down to the drugstore too."

Jennie wished he wouldn't. Roger in the office was one thing. Roger socially was another. But she said nothing. As it worked out, they walked to the corner and had a quiet snack with no unpleasantness at all.

The months wore on, and the corner drugstore became a habit. Once or twice a week, when they stayed late at the office, they went out for a sandwich. He frequently offered to drive her home, but she insisted on using the bus. It took her almost to her door, and he lived in the opposite direction.

This is where the matter stood one lovely day in May when she met Dotty Clements downtown during a quick noon-hour shopping trip, and they decided to have lunch together for old times' sake. After they were seated and lunch was ordered, Dotty lighted her customary cigarette. "What's new with you, Jen?" she asked with an impish grin.

"Nothing much," Jennie replied, "We've been working a lot of late hours since we received a large order in March."

"Yeah, I heard about you and your boss having dinner together." Dotty grinned knowingly. "You know, Jen, I always thought you were too good to be true." There was no malice in the remark, but Jennie was aghast at the implication. Not for one moment had she thought that such a conclusion could be put on her innocent snacks at the drugstore.

"Oh, Dotty, it's not like that at all!"

Dotty winked. "Hm-m, that's what they all say."

Jennie hated the implication and felt compelled to convince her happy-go-lucky friend. Her voice was shaking, but she tried in vain to make Dotty understand.

"I almost think you really believe, Jennie Shelby, that Roger Winters is taking you to dinner just to get you back to work sooner!" she chuckled.

"That *is* the reason!" Jennie insisted, almost in tears.

"Well, take it from me, *he* has something else in mind even if you don't. That old boy is a swinger, and don't you forget it!"

Jennie was trembling and sat silently staring at her plate. Her mind flew back over many little things Roger had said and done over the past few months. She had thought them merely thoughtful. Now she wondered. "Am I *that* gullible?"

The rest of the lunch hour was a blur, and as they were parting, she tried once more. Putting her hand on Dotty's arm she said, "Dotty, I wish I could convince you. Roger thinks of me only as an employee, an old family friend. Why, I have known his wife since we were little girls. Even if I were that kind of person, I wouldn't allow anything that would hurt her!"

Dotty hesitated. "Well, if you say so," she said with a shrug. "Oh, let's just forget it!"

They parted at the door, and Jennie, with head down and hands in her pockets, walked thoughtfully back to the office and a long afternoon.

The next few days were uneventful except that Jennie received a letter from her cousin in Oak Park, Illinois. Paul wrote only occasionally, but his letters were full of family happenings. He mentioned his new clinic. Jennie was too enmeshed in her own twisted affairs to pay much attention. She read the letter hastily, laying it aside to read again later. She missed entirely the last paragraph in which he told her that there would soon be a vacancy in his office, and if she had changed her mind, the job was hers.

Kathy had invited a few of her friends for dinner one evening to celebrate her twelfth birthday, after which they were to go on to a youth gathering at the church. The phone rang just as Jennie said goodbye to them, with a hug and a kiss for Kathy.

"Jennie, I want to talk to you." It was Eileen's voice, and she sounded as though she had been crying.

"Eileen! Are you all right?"

"I don't really know," came the reply in a voice shaking with emotion, "but I must talk to you as soon as possible."

"Sure, Honey, any time you say. Should I come out there?"

"No, I'll come to see you. Will you be home for a while?"

"Yes, of course." Jennie started to say more, but the line went dead, and she realized that Eileen had hung up.

"Oh dear, what now?" she asked herself as she hurried to clear up the kitchen.

It took Eileen just under half an hour to arrive, instead of her usual forty-five minutes. Jennie greeted her and offered a piece of birthday cake, but Eileen refused.

"Sit down, Jennie," she said. "This is not going to be easy for me."

Jennie sank into a chair while Eileen paced the room. Turning, she stood, her eyes blazing with anger. "Jen, how could you?"

Jennie's throat was dry. "What do you mean?" she said almost in a whisper.

"You know very well what I mean," Eileen snapped. "Just because you lost your husband, do you have to take someone else's?"

Jennie's mind froze. "Oh, Honey, please tell me what you heard."

Eileen's glance was full of venom. "So you can say it isn't true? I have put up with Roger's affairs for years, and I can't stand any more. I'm going to leave him!"

Jennie was numb. Beginning at the beginning, she tried to explain exactly what had happened, but Eileen sullenly turned her face away and said, "I don't believe a word you've said. I'm going to leave him!"

"Is there anything I can say or do that will make you know that this is not what you think?" Jennie begged.

Eileen looked her right in the eye. "Yes, leave town. Give up your cushy job and go back where you belong!"

Jennie was stunned, but before she could answer, Eileen picked up her purse and slammed out the door.

Jennie felt weighted down with dread as she entered the office the next Monday morning, but she kept reminding herself of the pastor's text the day before. He had read Romans 8:28: "We know that all things work together for good to them that love God, to them who are the called according to his purpose." She kept repeating the words in her mind.

How the Lord could bring anything good out of this mess she didn't know, but faith meant trusting, and she was trying.

Roger came storming in about eleven without his customary "good morning," and went into his office, shutting the door. It wasn't long until the buzzer sounded and he asked Jennie to "come in here."

Gathering pencil, pad, and the mail, she went.

He was sitting with his back to her, staring out the window behind his desk. She sat quietly until he turned around, his face like a thunder cloud.

"My wife is a fool! A dad-blasted fool! She's leaving me!" He spoke through gritted teeth.

Jennie sighed, "Yes, I know. She came to see me Saturday."

"She *what?*" He bolted out of his chair and began to pace the floor. "It's really my fault. She's right about my affairs, but they didn't mean a thing." He coughed and turned and looked at Jennie.

"I may as well tell you that I hired you away from Jim Ingersoll as a bet. He said you were straight and could not be touched, and I bet him you could, if I handled you right." He shrugged and resumed his pacing. "Blast it, Jennie, every time I started to make a pass, you quoted Scripture or something." He paced some more. "Anyway you've been a good secretary, and I didn't want to lose you. Maybe we can work something out."

They talked in circles for a while, and then he suggested that they take the rest of the day off and try again the next day.

It was a very troubled and confused Jennie that went home that day. She couldn't throw off the feeling that nothing would be the same in the office again. What should she do?

Chapter 12
Oak Park

Jennie reviewed the shocking events of the past few days in her mind that evening as she finished the kitchen chores. She heard the phone ring, but since most calls these days were for Kathy anyway, she paid no attention until she heard Kathy call her name. "Mother, it's for you. Long distance. Hurry!"

Drying her hands hastily, Jennie hurried to the phone. "Hello?"

"Hi, Jen, what's new?" her cousin Paul's voice boomed over the line.

Jennie caught her breath. He had written her, and she hadn't answered! "Oh, Paul," she exclaimed, "I'm sorry I didn't answer your letter, but I've been just swamped. Is everyone all right?"

"Sure. I mainly called to ask if you want the job."

"Job?"

"Yes, the one I wrote about in the letter."

Jennie gasped and nearly dropped the phone. "I, er, I'm not sure I understand," she said, her voice just above a whisper.

"I'm sure I asked you if you'd be interested in a job as office manager in my new pediatric clinic when I wrote," he said. "I've been expecting you to call."

"I'm sorry, Paul," Jennie replied sheepishly. "I had just been through a very painful experience when your letter arrived, and I must have missed that part." She paused. "It's interesting that you should call just now, though. I'm very interested in your offer. Can you spare me another twenty-four hours to think it over and talk to Kathy?"

"Sure thing. When could you let me know?"

"How about tomorrow evening at suppertime?"

72

"Good! I'll wait for your call." They chatted a bit about family details, and as Jennie hung up, a feeling of complete peace washed over her. "So this is the Lord's way of 'making all things work together for good.' " She felt very humble and bowed her head and said quietly, "Thank You, Lord."

It was with a feeling of dread that she broached the subject with Kathy later that evening. Although she had not told her about the fiasco at the office, she found the girl much more open than she had hoped.

"When would we go?" Kathy asked thoughtfully.

Jennie explained the things that had to be taken care of and that it would take a month or six weeks.

"Good! I'll have time to finish my swimming lessons."

"Are you disappointed?" Jennie asked.

"No, not really. But, Mom, can't we stay in the same place when I get into high school?"

Jennie pulled her into her arms and kissed her. "I sincerely hope we can stay put for many, many years," she whispered affectionately.

It was amazing how smoothly everything seemed to move as they said their goodbyes, went to farewell luncheons, and made arrangements for the furniture to be moved. Paul provided the moving expenses so Jennie didn't even have to do her own packing. What a difference from the move to Sioux City! She ran the comparison through her mind many times during those last few weeks.

As they boarded the plane for Chicago, Jennie realized that her only real regret about leaving was Roger's sullen farewell. He had done everything he could to persuade her to stay. Eileen had called to say, in a cool and very unconvincing voice, that Jennie really didn't need to go after all. Jennie was saddened to know that she had probably lost a lifelong friend, and she prayed that time would heal those wounds.

The first few weeks in Oak Park were very busy, with learning a new job, finding a new school for Kathy, and hunting for an apartment that was conveniently located to both. They chose a church some distance away, but there was good bus service. Jennie had managed without a car during her entire time in Sioux

City, and she insisted to Paul that she could as easily get along without one in Illinois, but he was equally insistent that she should have one, that he'd help her get one and see that she didn't go bankrupt paying for it. "I'll even advise you on repairs so you won't get stuck with some jerk that tries to hold up a woman," he laughed.

So she agreed. Paul helped her to find a used Honda Accord that looked like new. Kathy clapped her hands and begged to learn how to drive.

Month followed month as they adjusted to new places and friends. Their new church was larger than the one in Sioux City and had a more active youth group. Kathy was becoming a delightful young lady with her vivacious nature and quick smile. She wore her hair shoulder length. Her large, dark blue eyes were fringed with long black lashes and sparkled with merriment most of the time. Jennie deferred to her judgment as much as possible, and they grew to enjoy one another more and more.

One of the highlights of the first months at Oak Park was the fact the Jennie was again asked to teach a Sunday School class. This time she took no chances. She went to the pastor with her story. He listened graciously.

"Thank you for telling me, Mrs. Shelby," he said, "but I'm sure this will make no difference." He smiled kindly. "Several years ago this became an immediate problem in the church, so I made an exhaustive study of the Scriptures on the subject. Of course, all Christians should avoid divorce, but in a case like yours, where there was no alternative and the marriage vows were broken by adultery, we believe the Bible absolves the innocent party and you are free to remarry. If that is the case, then you should be equally free to serve in any leadership for which you are qualified, whether married or single. If you're free, you're free. This is the position we take."

The Sunday School class was a real joy. The study and prayer she needed to prepare the lessons fed her own soul and sweetened her relationship with the Lord.

When life is busy and happy, the years pass unnoticed. As Jennie surveyed herself in the mirror one morning she realized, with a shock, that her fortieth birthday was only a few days away. Where had the years gone? Glancing in the mirror again, she saw a slender, dark-haired woman who didn't look forty—at least she didn't feel forty.

The four years since they had come to Oak Park had been very rewarding years and had gone by so quickly. Kathy had just celebrated her sixteenth birthday, and now Jennie faced her fortieth. She sighed. Just two more years and her daughter would finish high school. What then? Jennie snapped her mind back to the present and finished dressing. She must be at the office in a few minutes, but it was walking distance and took only about ten minutes.

This morning, covering the short distance through a pleasant part of town, she was thinking about her own future.

Her life was very pleasant, but she wondered if this was all the Lord had for her. Her thoughts often went to the scripture she had claimed so many years ago: "thou shalt forget the shame of thy youth, and shalt not remember the reproach of thy widowhood any more." Somehow she had vaguely thought this Bible verse was a promise that she would someday remarry. She unlocked the clinic and hurried into her office. "Well, time will tell," she thought as she sat down at her desk.

Afterward it was to seem almost like one of life's little miracles that she should meet Jim Clark the very next day. Pastor Riley's duties became too heavy for one man to carry alone. So the church asked a younger man to take over some of the visiting and teaching.

Jim Clark had been a member of a nationally known dance band and a heavy drinker. One night, on the verge of suicide, he met a young man in a restaurant who started a conversation that eventually led Jim to accept Christ as Saviour and turn his life around. He attended Bible school at the age of forty-five and now had come as Pastor Riley's assistant.

That evening Jennie had gone to the church library for help with her coming Sunday School lesson. Kathy had recently learned to drive and had passed her driver's examination. Jennie had agreed to let her have the car for the evening for a church-sponsored youth function. "Just drop me off at the church," she had said. "I'll catch a ride home on the bus."

But when Jennie stepped out of the church she discovered that it was raining heavily. She stepped back inside, waiting till the worst was over before dashing to the bus stop, when Pastor Riley and Jim Clark came into the vestibule.

"Don't you have an umbrella, Jennie?" Pastor Riley asked.

"I never have one when I need it," she admitted, "and when I do have one I usually lose it!"

They all laughed. Pastor Riley glanced at the heavy rain. "Well, I have to keep an appointment in the opposite direction from your home," he said, "but Jim can take you home, I'm sure." He glanced at his assistant, who had no choice but to say that he would be glad to.

After they were in the car she apologized for the inconvenience, and of course he said he didn't mind. From then on the conversation was stilted.

She thanked him again after they drove up in front of her apartment, and started to get out, but Jim pulled her back into the car and began to laugh. She was puzzled, but smiled and asked, "Did I say something funny?"

"No, but we both seem so stiff and uncomfortable, and what you don't know is that I have been trying to think of a graceful way to get to know you ever since I came. Then, human nature being what it is, I was a little indignant when things were taken out of my hands."

"Oh?" she raised her brows. "I'm not all that hard to get to know, really." After a few minutes of relaxed conversation, he invited her to go to a concert at the Opera House in Chicago the following week. To her own surprise, she accepted.

Kathy was intrigued at this new development, but with a furrowed brow she asked, "Mother have you really *looked* at Pastor Jim? He's kinda creepy looking."

Jennie's dark brows flew up. "What do you mean?"

"We-l-l," the girl said slowly, "he's almost bald, and well—just kinda ugly. He seems so *old!* You're just too young and pretty for him," she finished lamely.

Jennie chuckled, cradling Kathy's face in her hands. "Don't worry, Honey. This is far from permanent."

However, their friendship grew, and Jennie began to realize how much nicer everything is when shared. Yet there was always a reserve in her manner, and Pastor Jim seemed strange and withdrawn at times. They talked of many things: music, which was his great love; the work he was doing in Oak Park; and Scripture. He had been a Christian only a short time, and he was still amazed by the wonder and fullness of God's Word. He had memorized great portions of it and seemed never to tire of talking about it. Something was missing in their relationship, however, and Jennie scolded herself for not being able to really relax in his presence.

Kathy said no more, but Jennie knew that she frankly did not like Pastor Jim. This troubled Jennie and made her more reticent with him.

After about three months, people at the church were aware of their friendship and began inviting them out as a couple. Yet Jennie felt troubled knowing that Kathy was not pleased. "I'd better decide just where this is heading," she told herself. This was the first time she had allowed any relationship to develop since the episode with Mike so many years before. She was very determined that a Christian should not be unequally yoked. Jim was a Christian, which made a difference, but somehow the spark was not there. Surely the Lord would give her a different feeling if this was a part of his perfect plan.

Just as she was prepared to bring up the matter with Jim, he took his vacation and went East to visit relatives. Kathy and Jennie were both relieved when he returned bringing a small, plain woman whom he introduced as his fiancée.

They had a good laugh together about it. "That does it," Jennie exclaimed. I'm going to be absolutely unapproachable from now on!"

"Oh, no, Mother!" Kathy replied quickly. "I wish you would marry again, but not someone like that!"

Jennie was surprised. "Do you really feel that way, Honey?"

"I will never get married if you don't," Kathy said firmly with the assurance of youth.

Now Jennie was shocked. This was the first time her daughter had ever expressed herself on the subject of her marriage.

"Do you *really* feel that way, Honey?" she asked.

"Oh, yes, Mother. I will never marry if you don't," she said firmly.

"Why do you say that?"

"You have given all your time and love to me all these years, and I just will not leave you—ever—unless you are married."

Jennie was amazed. Had Kathy thought this all out alone? "You must feel that you have been a burden, Kathy. You have been only joy to me, and I want you to have a full and normal life."

Kathy was silent for a moment. "I know, Mother, but I just could not leave you alone, and I won't marry anyone who won't take you too," she insisted.

Jennie laughed, but her heart swelled with pride and love. "That's very sweet, and I know you mean well, but what if I don't want to live with you? What if I don't like your husband?"

"Then I won't marry him!" Kathy said stubbornly.

Jennie knew that when Kathy fell in love she would feel differently, but the teenager's loyalty was heartwarming. Jennie chuckled and shrugged. "Well, I'd better get married first, then; I can see that." And they both laughed.

The phone rang for Kathy, and she was caught up in the evening's plans, forgetting the conversation at once. But Jennie thought of it a long time. Later, lying in bed, she wondered what would happen when Kathy met a young man she loved. She had ceased to wrestle with the desire for marriage for herself. She was content to live out her years alone, if that was the Lord's will for her.

"Please work it out in your own way and time, Lord," she breathed as sleep claimed her.

Chapter 13
Don McMillan

Life had settled into a very pleasant routine, and the years passed so smoothly that Kathy was ready to graduate from high school before Jennie could catch her breath, it seemed. Where had the time gone? They enjoyed one another so much. They liked the same books, wore each other's clothes, and laughed at the same things. Now the time had come for Kathy to leave for nurse's training in Chicago.

Jennie was thinking about these things one evening when she was home alone. "I've known it was coming, and I've tried to prepare myself," she mused as she stirred up a batch of cookies in the kitchen. "But for the first time in many years I feel lonely and discontented." She squared her shoulders and promised herself not to give in to self-pity.

Jennie had removed the cookies from the oven and set them out to cool by the time Kathy came home. She found her mother in the finishing touches of setting the kitchen to rights. Jennie made a final swipe at some crumbs on the counter, then sat down at the kitchen table with Kathy to discuss the day, Kathy's plans for nurse's training, and her latest boyfriend.

"It's been a good life, Mother, thanks to you," Kathy said, reaching for one of the freshly baked cookies that Jennie had set out on a plate between them.

"I'm proud of you, Honey, as I always knew I would be. I want you to have everything the Lord has planned for you." She reached over and squeezed Kathy's hand. They looked into each other's eyes for a moment and smiled. Then each of them ate another cookie, and neither of them spoke for several minutes.

Finally Kathy yawned. "I'm going to get a bath and some sleep so I can get on with the business of living tomorrow without circles under my eyes."

The next week Kathy was in a whirl, filling out forms, packing, and taking care of endless details. There was a flurry of shopping, and then it was time to go.

They loaded all of Kathy's things into the car, and Jennie drove her daughter to the school in Chicago where she was to take her training. She met Kathy's new roommate and helped her move in and unpack her things. She managed to find excuses to stay till suppertime, when she took Kathy and her roommate out to eat.

But finally the time came when she had to leave. Kathy walked out to the parking lot with her mother. "What will you do evenings, Mother?" she asked as they stood by the car. "I'll worry about you."

"Don't you dare!" Jennie replied. "I'll read and do some sewing. I might even become a volunteer at the hospital. I've always wanted to do that."

"We can call each other up on the phone too," Kathy said. "And of course I'll be home for visits, although they say we don't get many breaks at first. Nothing for four weeks."

Four weeks without seeing Kathy sounded like a lifetime to Jenny, but she said nothing. They hugged and cried a little and bowed their heads for a short prayer. Then Jennie left, waving one last time as she turned the corner.

Thus began a new phase in Jennie's life. She felt rudderless. All her plans to keep busy seemed so senseless. With Kathy's friends no longer calling, the phone sat stubbornly silent, pouting on the desk. Each evening when she came home she flipped on the radio just to have the sound of a human voice in the apartment. Her meals became sketchy and uninteresting. "I must snap out of this and get involved in something," she scolded herself.

It was her need to keep busy that kept Jennie going to choir practice. She and Kathy had both been members of the choir, but after Kathy left Jennie thought she might give it up. She kept going just to have something to do.

Each night anyone who came for the first time was asked to stand and give his or her name. At the first practice in October, a new man in the bass section was asked to introduce himself. His name was Don McMillan. He said that he enjoyed the singing, but could not always attend the rehearsals. Jennie paid no attention to him except to note that he had a slight British accent and she had always been fascinated by accents. The incident completely escaped her mind, and the man did not return.

On Friday a couple of weeks later Jennie took her car to the garage for an oil change, and the mechanic pointed out a problem that needed immediate attention. "We can fix it if you can leave it over the weekend," he said. Jennie agreed, knowing that she could easily catch a bus to church.

Before the choir entered the church for the service the next Sunday morning, the director told the members that they were desperately short of men in the bass section. "We simply cannot use the music that I have chosen for our Thanksgiving program without a full bass section," he said. "Please, each of you, try to find more men who sing bass."

After Jennie was settled in her seat, she looked out over the congregation, and she noticed the same man who had been in choir practice two weeks earlier. She couldn't remember his name, but she thought someone should invite him to sing.

The service held her attention, so she gave the matter no more thought until she was shouldering her way through the crowd after church rather hurriedly to catch the 12:30 bus. Standing at the door, looking a little lost, was Don McMillan. Almost without thinking, Jennie went over and with a friendly smile put her hand out and said, "Hi, I'm Jennie Shelby. Aren't you the man who came to choir practice a few weeks ago?" She noticed that his face was very thin and etched with deep lines, as though he held some deep pain, but his smile was transforming. The even white teeth and the twinkle in his eyes completely erased the drawn look.

He shook her hand. "Yes, but I haven't been able to come back. My name is Don McMillan."

She glanced nervously at her watch. "We need basses desperately. Just this morning the choir director urged us to invite any man who can sing to join us." He seemed a little nervous, she thought.

"My work is pretty confining," he said. "Sometimes I work evenings and just can't get away."

"I must hurry, as I don't want to miss my bus," Jennie explained, searching in her purse for bus fare, "but do come next week if you can."

"Why not let me drive you home?" he said. "I have no plans for today."

Jennie looked at him. He seemed to be a nice enough person, clean and neat, and rather nice looking too, but he was a complete stranger, so she said No.

"I really would be glad to drive you," he said, "and I promise to take you right home."

Just then Jennie looked out the door and saw the bus pulling away from the curb. That meant a two-hour wait on Sundays! She shrugged, "I see that I just missed my bus, so I would appreciate a ride home."

It had all happened so fast that they were both a little embarrassed, but to keep the conversation going Jennie told him that she lived alone since her daughter had gone to nursing school and that Sunday afternoons were set aside for letter writing.

"I promised to take you right home," he said, "and I'll still do that if you wish. However, since you're alone and I'm alone, why not let me take you out to dinner? I'll take you anywhere you choose."

It had been so long since Jennie had been in the company of a man alone that she felt nervous. She had been hurt too many times, and besides, she knew nothing whatsoever about this man except that he came to church. On the other hand it would be a chance to avoid eating alone, and she knew a nice place where she and Kathy had often gone out to eat. "Surely I'm capable of handling this simple situation properly," she thought. But out loud she said, "Oh, I already have my lunch prepared at home, and I must write to Kathy this afternoon."

He didn't say anything for a block or two. Jenny almost wondered if he was upset that she had turned him down. A moment later he brought the car to a stop at a red light. Then he turned to her and said, "I'd really appreciate it if you would keep a lonely man from eating alone. I'll promise to take you home immediately, as soon as lunch is over."

He sounded so sincere, and Jennie really didn't want to go home to an empty apartment. "I guess I could do that," she said. "I know a nice little place over on Chicago Avenue."

"I would like to tell you a little about myself so that you will be at ease with me," he said after they were seated in a quiet corner and had each given the waitress an order. He related to her the story of a tragic marriage in which, from the first, his wife was unhappy and restless. She told him the first week that she only went through with the wedding because the invitations were out and she wanted to wear her beautiful wedding dress. All through their marriage she flaunted her affairs before him, and several times she left him. She kept demanding a divorce, but he wanted *her*. He finally enlisted in the navy to give her time to think. There had been a reconciliation, for he truly wanted the marriage to work. They even had a little boy, but the child was not strong and only lived two years.

Following the death of the child his wife went away with one of her men friends for a week, but came back pleading for forgiveness. They tried once more to make it work, but it was no use. One day he came home and found her in the arms of a neighbor. They quarreled violently. She demanded that he leave, and in complete disillusionment he complied. He made no effort to stop her when she filed for divorce.

Tortured and angry, he didn't know what to do, but he hated to admit defeat. He decided that even though he no longer loved her, if she changed her mind, he would take her back. However, soon after the divorce she married the neighbor, and they recently had a child.

That was where matters stood. Trying to build a new life, he was devoting most of his time to his business. He felt lonely, however, and quite out of place with his married friends.

Jennie understood how he felt, even though her hurt was now fourteen years away and seemed more like a vague dream than something that had actually happened. She briefly told him her story.

After dinner she agreed to a short ride in the country. Soon they began to feel relaxed in one another's company. Don dropped her off at her apartment in time for her to write a chatty letter to Kathy, though she did not mention her new friend.

That evening at church Jennie noticed that Don was again in the congregation. She determined to slip out the side door and catch the bus before he saw her. She certainly did not want him to think she expected him to drive her home again! Besides, she had heard all the sad stories she could take in one day.

As soon as evening service was dismissed, Jennie hurried out the side door and reached the bus stop without being seen. She waited in the shadows of a building, fare in hand, hoping he would not find her. She was startled by his voice as he materialized out of the darkness, hands in his pockets.

"It's obvious you are avoiding me, and I am wondering if I said something today to offend you."

"Oh, no, not at all!" she replied a little nervously. "It was a very interesting afternoon."

"Why don't you let me drive you home tonight?" he asked.

She glanced down the dark street. There was no bus in sight, nor could she think of a good reason to refuse. "Well, if you're sure it isn't out of your way," she said lamely.

It was a lovely October evening in spite of a slight chill in the air. They talked very little. Pulling up in front of her apartment house, Don said, "You really gave me a very interesting and pleasant day, and I want to thank you again."

She turned, opening the door to get out, but he continued, "How long will I have to know you before you invite me in?"

Jennie turned and looked at him. She decided that she was not very interested in knowing him better. "Probably never," she said frankly. "I've lived in this apartment building for almost six years, and I've never yet entertained a man alone. I realize that I am considered a prude, but my Christian example and appearance are very important to me." She stepped out on the sidewalk. "I've heard the remarks made about some of the single women who allow their men friends in their apartments day or night, and I want to be sure they can never say anything like that about me." Her voice was a little impatient. She said a brief good night and walked into the building.

"Shame on you, Jennie!" she thought. "You were very rude, and you sure spoiled that friendship." For some reason, though, she was too tired and bothered to care.

Chapter 14
The Persistent Suitor

Monday was always a busy day at the clinic, but that particular day was hectic. Three people were waiting when Jennie unlocked the office door. The doctors didn't arrive until around ten o'clock, but two nurses on the staff could bandage minor hurts and give shots. From the moment she sat down at her desk till time to go home, she was caught up in a rush of people with sore throats, upset stomachs, and an endless list of complaints. In the five years she had been there, the office staff had grown from two to six. She now had a private office in the back, but often had to go to the front to fetch a file or to settle a problem.

The receptionist called in to say that she had a migraine headache and couldn't come in. This meant that Jennie had to help with the phones and take payments in addition to keeping her own desk clear. All this to the accompaniment of crying babies and squabbling youngsters left her exhausted by the time she finally locked the door at the end of the day.

Back at the apartment that evening, Jennie had just finished her meager supper and settled into her favorite chair for the evening news when the phone rang. "It could be Kathy," she thought, but she was surprised to hear Don's voice instead.

"This has been a very strange day for me," he said after they had exchanged greetings. "I have not been able to get you out of my mind."

She was surprised, for she honestly hadn't thought of him at all. "Oh? I have had a very heavy day. There seems to be an epidemic of sore throats and upset stomachs going around."

He was solicitous. "I hope I'm not interrupting anything."

"No," she assured him, "I was just watching the news."

He plunged on. "I would like to see you again. Would it be an imposition if I came by and picked you up for a little ride?"

Jennie loved to ride, but at the moment she felt exhausted. Still she didn't want to be unkind. "I'm truly sorry," she said, "but I'm really too tired tonight. I'm afraid I wouldn't be very good company. Perhaps some other time." She told him that she remembered how it had helped her to talk over her heartaches, and she was grateful to those friends who had listened so many years ago, but right now she felt she just couldn't handle any more of his sad story.

"I feel that I need someone like you," he said, "a Christian girl, who can understand the situation I'm in."

"Honestly," she thought, "this is too much!" But to him she said, "I'll be glad to introduce you to several girls at church."

"I'm sorry," he said. "Maybe I'm being too forward, but I want to be sure you understand. I'm not interested in other girls. I'm interested in you."

Jennie caught her breath and wondered whether she should feel irritated or flattered. They talked a few more minutes, after which she asked to be excused as she really needed to go to bed. She kept thinking of their conversation, as she put on her night clothes. She always seemed to end on a sharp note with him, and she wondered why he persisted in calling her back. However, she put the matter out of her mind as soon as she turned out the light. Within minutes, she was fast asleep.

The next day at the clinic was a little less hectic, and Jennie came home feeling more like herself. She phoned Kathy, and they had a nice chat, so she was feeling in a happy mood when the phone rang.

"Hi, this is Jennie," she said cheerfully.

"Jennie, this is Don."

"Oh, hi Don. How did your day go?"

"Pretty good. Busy. I must apologize, though. I'm afraid I said all the wrong things last night." There was a moment's silence. "I would like to see you again, though. Could I pick you up for a ride tonight?"

Jennie paused. Should she or shouldn't she? She decided it couldn't hurt to go out with him one more time. He was, after all, a

Christian. "Why don't you pick me up, and we can go to McDonalds for a soft drink. Then maybe we can drive around a while?" she said.

"Good!" he replied. "I'll see you shortly."

Ten minutes later she heard a gentle knock at the door. Jennie picked up her coat, opened the door, and let Don help her put it on.

They ordered french fries and milkshakes and talked of unimportant things. In the car again, he took the freeway a short distance to an upper-class section of town with beautiful homes. They parked under a street light in front of a ball park where a group of junior boys were playing softball—"Probably Little League," Jennie thought. She wondered whether Don had chosen this place because it was public and therefore safe from criminals or because he wanted to avoid frightening her about his own intentions. Either way, she appreciated the fact that they were not alone in some dark part of the city.

They laughed at the children's play for several minutes. Then Don leaned over as though to talk about something more serious. "I know that I spent all of our time last Sunday telling you about my troubles," he said, "and that was a mistake. I realize that I have brooded too much about it. I can see that I have created quite a lot of self-pity for myself which is wrong. Now I want to tell you some of the more pleasant things about myself. So that you can know me as I really am." He launched into an account of his life.

His birthplace had been Scotland. His parents brought their sons to America during the early forties because work in the war industries was so plentiful. Most of his younger years he spent in New Jersey, till he enlisted in the navy. After college he signed up with a major construction firm as an engineer. However, the breakup of his marriage drove him so near to emotional and physical collapse that, on his doctor's advice, he took a job as a construction worker, where the mental strain would not be so great. This work interested him more than he had ever imagined, and in due time he started up his own construction firm. "It's a fairly new business," he said, "but it's doing amazingly well. The Lord has been good."

Their eyes met. What she saw startled her at first—not what she saw in his eyes but what she saw in her own heart. She almost gasped, and for an instant she wanted to look away, but she couldn't. For his eyes told her that she had found what she had been looking for all these years. She had dreamed about a man holding her in his arms, yet at this moment that didn't matter at all. She felt no impulse to move closer to him. She just knew, and the knowing moved her deeply.

"I understand," she said in a whisper so low that she wondered if he heard. He nodded, and they smiled.

Later, as they walked slowly back to her apartment, he told her that he had a dinner meeting the next evening, but he suggested that on Thursday he pick her up after work so they could have dinner together before choir practice. They parted with a hand clasp and plans to meet in two days.

As Jennie prayed that night, she said, "Lord, thank You for a new friend, but You know how gullible I am. Please don't let me depend too much on this friendship."

Wednesday evening Jennie went to midweek service. Afterward, the phone was ringing as she walked into the apartment. It was Don. He said he just wanted to hear her voice and tell her about his evening. He had been to a Christian businessmen's meeting. "Good food, good speaker, and good fellowship," he said, "but I missed seeing you." They talked briefly, and when Jennie hung up her heart was singing. "How nice for him to call just to share his pleasure! What's happening to me?" she thought.

She was too excited to sleep, so she washed and set her hair and did her nails. "I feel giddy as a teenager," she thought. Lying in bed, she went over the events since the previous Sunday, cautioning herself not to make too many plans or imagine a lot of things that were not there. He might lose interest by this time next week, or perhaps she would. After all, she had known him less than a week! She got out of bed, knelt down, and prayed.

"Lord, please don't let me make a fool of myself again. I truly want Your will. I am content to live my life alone, if that is Your plan for me. Please bless Don, and heal his hurt in Your way and in Your time. Amen."

Her heart quieted and she slept, deeply, and without dreams.

Chapter 15
The Lord's Doing

Thursday Jennie's heart was light all day. That evening she would see Don again. Early in the afternoon the phone rang at the clinic, and Jennie picked it up almost automatically. However, she came to life instantly when she heard Kathy's voice at the other end of the line.

"Mother, guess what! I have a few hours off on Sunday and I can come home!"

"Wonderful!" Jennie exclaimed. "How will you get here?"

"On the El," Kathy replied, and she told her mother when to meet her.

Don had told her that he would call before the afternoon was up and tell her when to expect him to arrive at her apartment. His call came at four o'clock, and Jennie thought she heard a note of excitement in his voice.

"I can't meet you quite as early as I had planned," he said. "I guess we'll have to miss choir practice. Can I pick you up around seven? We can go on a ride again and talk. I have something very important to tell you."

"What is it?" she asked.

"You'll find out," he said.

"Hm-m, sounds mysterious. I can't wait."

Don laughed and hung up.

The doorbell rang promptly at seven. When she opened the door, Don placed a beautiful bouquet of white roses in her arms.

"Ooo!" she exclaimed. "They're lovely!"

"White represents purity," he said.

Jennie felt the tears rush to her eyes, and for a minute she couldn't talk. She looked into his eyes and smiled. "Thank you," she said.

Don reached for her hand and squeezed it, led her to the car, and opened the door. "Well, where would you like to drive this evening?" he asked after they were seated and had buckled their seat belts.

She thought a minute. "I've always enjoyed Lake Shore Drive, with all those beautiful homes on one side and the lake on the other."

They drove to a quiet spot where they could look out over the lake. Then Don turned and looked at her. "I have several things I want to say," he told her with a twinkle in his eye, "and I want you to just listen and not say anything until I am through, no matter how surprised you are."

She laughed.

He took a deep breath—almost as though he were trying to quiet the nerves in his stomach, Jennie thought.

"First, I must tell you that I am in love with you," he said. "From the minute you walked out onto the choir loft last Sunday morning, I *knew* you were the answer to my prayer. It was like a spotlight was focused on you, and the assurance was there. He paused and took another breath. "I'm a little embarrassed, at my age, to go around accosting women, so before I left for church that day I asked the Lord to let someone speak to me, and if He had a wife for me, to let her speak to me first." Don paused again and looked into Jennie's eyes. "Do you remember how we met?"

Jennie felt her heart racing. She had spoken to him casually, almost on an impulse, inviting him to join the choir. "I had no romantic intentions in my head, honest," she said quietly.

"I know you didn't," Don replied. "That's what's so exciting about this whole thing. This is God's doing, not ours!"

"It almost frightens me," Jennie said.

Don continued talking, almost as though he hadn't heard. "The next thing I must tell you is that I want you to marry me," he said.

Jennie gasped.

Don smiled. "I'm serious. The reason I couldn't pick you up earlier this evening is that I wanted to talk to Pastor Riley. I wanted him to know my intentions, and I also wanted his advice and blessing, since he knows my troubles, and I think he knows something about yours. He was very kind. He said he felt that we were both free to remarry, and if you could love me, too, he saw no reason for us not to go ahead. He did caution that we should not move too rapidly."

Jennie had been looking at her lap as Don spoke. She opened her mouth, but the words wouldn't come. She shook her head, and then looked into his face. "I—I—I don't know," she said. "What will people think?" She no more than said the words then she regretted them. At a moment like this, what did it matter what others thought? But Don was still talking.

"Pastor Riley said that we might find some people in church who still are not willing to allow marriage after divorce, and we must be prepared to accept that without feeling hurt. It will take time and compassion on our part, and some people may never change their minds. But he said that this is a private, personal matter between us and the Lord."

In all the years she had waited and wondered, Jennie had never dreamed of anything like the moment she was just now experiencing. It was as though she were in a trance, in another world, where reality was something totally different from what she was accustomed to here in Chicago. Had anyone told her a week ago that she would be sitting in a car tonight listening to a man propose marriage to her, she would have told them they were crazy; and had the idea entered her head that she would remain seated in the car seriously considering his proposal she would have called herself crazy. Yet here she was, listening to those very words and feeling utterly thrilled and awed.

She looked up, and he was smiling. "Well, what do you think?" he said, with a twinkle in his eye. "Am I crazy? I know I've shocked you. I went out to see my folks this afternoon and told them all about you and that I plan to marry you no matter how long I have to wait. Of course, they think I'm cracking up too." Then his voice took on a serious note. "Truly, I am very sincere, Jennie. I know how sudden this is. Maybe it's even childish, I don't know. But I'm so sure of how I feel about you that I decided not to waste another precious minute to tell you. But I will wait as long as you need in order to be sure."

By now Jennie had regained some of her composure, though she felt herself trembling inside. She wondered if Don could tell.

"Thank you," she said, hoping that her voice didn't tremble too. "It's wonderful. Truly wonderful—the idea, I mean. But I hardly know you! We have only seen each other a couple of times this week. This time last week I barely knew you existed."

He sobered. "I know, Jennie, that this is very sudden, but that's the way it hit me when you walked out into that choir loft. I have not doubted since then that this is from the Lord. Of course, my common sense tells me we have to be very sure. I guess it was the little boy in me that made me want to shock you." He reached over and put his big hand over her folded ones in her lap. "It has to be mutual, Jennie, and I will make no demands, but I do love you with all my heart. It makes me feel like a kid again!"

Jennie didn't look at him when she spoke. She kept her eyes fixed on her hands. She faltered for her first words. "I guess, well, I don't know. I can't say that I love you. For me, that would take more time. But I can say this, that you are, as far as I can tell, the kind of man I *could* love." She looked into his face and smiled. "I'm willing to give our friendship time and see if I can." She looked at her hands again. "It's very flattering that you should ask me to marry you, and I can honestly say that from the way everything looks right now I hope it works out that way. It would fulfill a lot of dreams. But I must pray about it."

Neither of them said anything for several minutes, yet the silence did not make Jennie feel nervous, nor did she feel that Don was uncomfortable. "It's strange," she thought, "how very comfortable I am with this man when I've known him for such a short time." She had not expected it to be this way. This seemed a good indication that they could make a good marriage together.

Don broke the silence. He began speaking slowly, deliberately. "I have given this a lot of thought, and I believe the reason the Lord brought us together was because we have had a similar experience with unwanted divorce. He expects us to approach remarriage very carefully. So let's relax and get to know one another. I want to make up to you all the lonely years and suffering you have been through. I believe the Lord will bless us."

They talked about his work and hers. She told him about Kathy and how very important her opinion would be. "I have not even told her that I met you," she laughed. "Until tonight I didn't think it was that important."

Later they stopped at a pizza place for a bite to eat. They got out of the car laughing and chattering, their hearts light as though they were children. As they approached the building, he held the door, and she gave her skirt a special swirl as she stepped through ahead of him. She held her head high, proudly, as though every customer in the place had their eyes fixed on her, admiring the wonderful man she was with. She had always felt a little ashamed of being with Mike, as though people wondered why *she* was with *him*. This was so different—so wonderfully different!

Somehow Jennie didn't mind that it took them far longer to finish their pizza that evening than it ever should have. She didn't feel nervous anymore. Just deliciously happy, looking into his eyes, holding his hand across their small table. "Love is being comfortable," she thought. "It's being happy in his presence." She remembered all the times she'd dreamed about love as a surge of passion. In one short hour her understanding of love had changed so dramatically, yet this was far more wonderful than any of her dreams.

They made their way to her apartment slowly. She teased him about taking the long way home. They drew up in front of her apartment, and he opened the door. "I still feel that my plan not to have you up to my apartment is best," she said as they walked to her door. "The Bible says to avoid the very appearance of evil, and I want to keep my standards high. When Kathy is home you can come, or we can invite another couple." They had reached her door by now, and she turned and looked up into his face.

"That's why I love you," he said softly. "I loved it when you were so spunky with me about your convictions."

Suddenly, without his even asking, as though it were the most natural thing in the world, she stepped into his arms and rested the side of her head against his chest. He held her close. His kiss was tender and brief. Letting her go, he held her at arm's length and said hoarsely, "I love you, Jennie, but we will wait until you feel as sure about this as I am."

She looked up with tears in her eyes. "Be patient with me, please."

He smiled and nodded.

Later, in the apartment, she prepared for bed in a daze. She sat on her bed with her Bible open on her lap and read the words of the promise that God had given her years before.

"Fear not; for thou shalt not be ashamed: neither be thou confounded; for thou shalt not be put to shame: for thou shalt forget the shame of thy youth, and shalt not remember the reproach of thy widowhood any more."

Tears filled her eyes till she could hardly see, but she didn't need to see the words to read them. Long ago she had memorized them, and she could read them on the screen in her mind as easily as she could read them from the page in front of her. "Thou shalt forget the shame of thy youth, and shalt not remember the reproach of thy widowhood any more."

She sank to her knees beside the bed. "Oh, thank you, precious Lord," she murmured.

Jennie was waiting on the El platform when Kathy's train pulled in on Sunday afternoon and the two women fell into one another's arms.

"You look so grown up, Honey!" Jennie exclaimed, eyeing this very attractive young woman who was her daughter.

"You look beautiful!" Kathy replied.

They chatted excitedly as they walked arm-in-arm the two blocks to her car.

"Mother, what have you done to yourself?" Kathy exclaimed as they settled down in the apartment for a good talk. "You simply glow! I don't think I've seen you so exuberant in all my life as you are this afternoon."

Jennie took a deep breath and launched into an account of the last week's happenings, explaining that she had not mentioned it before because she had not thought it important at first. "But after last Thursday night!" she exclaimed. She went into detail about everything, from the time she stopped Don and invited him to sing in the choir, until that morning. Her heart beat faster, for it was so important that Kathy approve. Their friendship simply could not progress any farther until she did.

Kathy's eyes grew wider and wider, but Jennie could only tell that she was amazed—dumbfounded. She could not tell what she was thinking by the look on her face. At last, Jennie finished her story, but she didn't ask Kathy what she thought. She just sat and waited.

Kathy sat speechless for a moment, staring at her mother, her mouth open wide. Then she sprang to her feet and flew across the room into her mother's arms. "Oh, Mother, how romantic!" she exclaimed. "When do I get to meet this Lochinvar?"

Jennie explained that Don would come over as soon as she called him.

"Well," Kathy said, "what are you going to tell him? Are you going to marry him?"

Jennie sobered. "I think so. Everything feels right, but of course we need time to get to know one another, so it will not be for a while. I want you to approve, and we need to take him to Crestview to meet our family. We must meet his family, and there are a lot of things we need to talk over. We both realize that this will be for the rest of our lives, and we don't want to rush it. Marriage should never be done in haste, even as sure as we both are. I think it will probably be a year. I didn't sleep last night thinking and praying about it."

Kathy nodded and slipped an arm around her mother as she continued.

"It is so strange how the Lord has worked in my life, Jennie said. "When your father deserted us so long ago, I was crushed and bitter. I wanted to be married so badly, but the Lord just gave me no opportunities. No doubt He knew how rebellious I felt inside. He took us away from Crestview, away from our family, and put us in a situation where I was forced to depend on Him completely.

"Gradually, I accepted my life as it was and even gloried in my independence. The last several years I have been very content. Life has been good, and I have accepted the fact that I might never get married again. And now this!" She spread her hands. "Last night I couldn't help but think of the story in the Bible where God asked Abraham to sacrifice his only son, Isaac, but when he was willing and had built an altar, the Lord didn't allow him to go through with it, but provided a more fitting sacrifice. Maybe the Lord just wanted me to be as willing as Abraham was. I don't know, but I do know that I feel good about this whole situation. It seems like the right thing to do."

They were sitting on the couch facing one another; Kathy leaned over and hugged her mother. "It couldn't have happened to a more deserving person," she whispered. They held each other for a few more seconds, and then Kathy leaned back and held her mother's shoulders at arm's length. "Now let's call Don," she said with a smile.

Later that evening, as the soft dusk crept over Oak Park and street lights began to blink on here and there, Jennie and Kathy and Don walked slowly along the platform of the El station. They heard a rumble in the distance, and a few seconds later the train rolled in and ground to a stop.

Kathy kissed her mother goodbye, and then looked at Don. "Wow!" she said. "You're one hunk of a man!" She hugged him briefly, then looked at him again, up and down, as though she were surveying him for quality. "It's sure going to be great having a dad around the house after all these years!" she exclaimed, and then she turned and ran to the train. She threw them each a kiss as the train pulled away.

Don glanced down at Jennie, his eyes sparkling. "Does that mean what I hope it does?" he asked.

Jennie's heart was in her eyes as she looked up at him. "It means that she approves, which is the first step." She grinned impishly. "Now we can move carefully as the Lord leads." She took his hand, and they walked slowly back to his car.

They rode in silence for several blocks. Then he looked over at her. "A penny for your thoughts."

"Is that all?" she teased. "They're worth a *lot* more than that."

"My checking account's kind of low right now," he said. "I guess that about the only thing I have left to offer is me."

"That'll do," she said as she slid over and leaned against his side. She rested her head on his shoulder. "I was just thinking of the verse in the Bible that says, 'This is the Lord's doing; it is marvellous in our eyes.' " Psalm 118:23.